David Collins is one of investigative reporters. In 2c journalist in the history of the ~~British Press Awards to win~~ News Reporter of the Year for helping police convict the serial killer Levi Bellfield for the murder of Milly Dowler. He joined *The Sunday Times* as an investigative reporter in 2015. Initially working as deputy editor of the Insight investigations team, his work exposed doping by Russian athletes in the World Championships and Olympic Games. The investigation won Sports Scoop of the Year and Best Investigative Team of the year at the Sports Journalism Awards in 2015. Other investigations include: an investigation into war crimes by British special forces in Afghanistan; and the murder of Agnes Wanjiru in Kenya (which won David and Hannah Al-Othman the Paul Foot Award for Investigative and Campaigning Journalism in 2022). He is currently northern editor for *The Sunday Times,* based in Manchester. His first book, *The Hunt for the Silver Killer,* was published in May 2022 by Simon & Schuster.

SAFFIE

*The youngest victim of
the Manchester terror attack
and her family's fight for justice*

David Collins
with Andrew and Lisa Roussos

SILVERTAIL BOOKS ◇ *London*

We dedicate this book to our beautiful, sweet, kind and loving Saffie. We are truly blessed to have you as our precious little girl. You filled our hearts with so much love and light. A light so bright and warm that it will shine forever.

Grief is simply love that has nowhere to go and we will carry it with us for an eternity.

Andrew and Lisa Roussos

Chapter 1
Pick Up

8.45pm, 22 May, 2017
The sun was going down when Andrew Roussos began to lock up his fish and chip shop after a typically slow Monday night. He switched off the neon OPEN sign in the front window and looked across the road, where two men and a woman were outside the pub opposite having a pint and breathing cigarette smoke into the warm evening air. Andrew turned and went back into the kitchen to make up three sausage butties. He wrapped them in paper and wrote "Saffie" on the sandwich without ketchup.

Saffie – Saffie-Rose Roussos – was Andrew's eight-year-old daughter, a chatterbox who was currently at a pop concert with her mother, Lisa, and who hated ketchup. He drew a love heart next to Saffie's name and popped the sandwiches into a plastic carrier bag. Then he checked his watch. 9pm.

Chrissy, one of Andrew's employees, was mopping the floor beside him. "She won't sleep tonight," Chrissy warned with a smile. "No chance."

Andrew and his wife Lisa had run The Plaice, a traditional English chippy on the corner of Hough Lane in Leyland, a small Lancashire town surrounded by peat fens, green fields and dairy farms, for five years. After a lot of

1

hard work, they now had just enough extra money to pay for presents for the children, family day trips, and holidays abroad.

The team who worked there were close and knew the family well. Along with most of the workers in the shop, Chrissy had a soft spot for Saffie. She called her "Princess". But Saffie hated it. She wanted to be a dancer, a pop singer or a TV actor. *Anything* but a princess.

Saffie wasn't exactly what you might call a girly girl. She enjoyed dressing up in nice clothes and looking pretty, but she hated dolls, and much preferred physical activities like getting mucky, climbing trees, and doing gymnastics. Her favourite Disney film was Mulan, about a girl pretending to be a boy in order to join the army, which just about summed her up.

Jan, another shop worker, walked in through the back door where she had been emptying the kitchen bins. "Any news from Saffie?" she asked.

"Lisa's been sending videos from the concert. Looks like she's having the time of her life," Andrew said.

"Aw, bless her."

The shop seemed eerily quiet without Saffie bouncing about, singing and dancing. One of her favourite tricks was to leap out of a cardboard box to scare Chrissy. Andrew and Jan would double up with laughter when they saw Chrissy jump out of her skin. Saffie seemed to catch her out every single time.

Andrew was working his way through his jobs as quickly

as he could so he could close the shop. He had one more call to make, to the fishmonger. He ordered three boxes of cod for the next day, then opened a door in the shop kitchen where a flight of stairs led up to the family home, a three-bedroom apartment which they had renovated and modernised when they bought the business.

"Xander?" Andrew called. "Come on, time to go."

"Coming," came the reply.

"Grab Binky, will you?"

Xander, Andrew and Lisa's 11-year-old son, appeared at the top of the stairs carrying Binky, the family's ginger and white Chihuahua, who suffered from a bad case of small-dog syndrome. Once she got to know you, she was a darling, but until then, she would bare her little teeth as ferociously as she could manage and bark her tiny head off whenever she saw you.

Tonight, Andrew and Xander were on pick up duty. Roughly thirty miles away, in Manchester city centre, the American pop star Ariana Grande was on stage at the Manchester Arena, a large concert venue next to Victoria train station. Lisa had gone with Saffie and Ashlee, Lisa's 25-year-old daughter from a previous marriage.

Saffie was a huge Ariana Grande fan. Her pictures and posters were all over Saffie's room, torn from magazines. Ashlee, on the other hand, was more into thrash metal and hard rock than pop music, but she loved going to live music concerts and wanted to be there for Saffie's big night out.

The family's dark-blue Jeep Cherokee was parked on the

pavement outside the shop. Xander got into the front passenger seat, Binky on his lap. He was still wearing his school uniform: the red polo shirt and dark trousers of Tarleton Community Primary School.

Andrew was in his black work T-shirt and a pair of combat trousers. He was a tall man at six feet two inches, with thick and dark greying hair, olive skin, and a trimmed goatee. Saffie used to say he looked like Mr Bean, a comparison Lisa found hilarious. Andrew didn't see the resemblance.

"Ready to see your sister?" Andrew said, turning the key in the ignition.

"I don't know why she even likes her," Xander muttered.

"Who?"

"Ariana Grande. She's rubbish."

Xander knew how to wind his sister up. All he had to do was say Selena Gomez was better than Ariana Grande. *Mum! Dad! Xander's ANNOYING me!* They made good time down the M61 motorway, then along the A580, driving past the tree-lined streets of Worsley into Salford, and across a bridge over the River Irwell. Andrew took a left down Hunts Bank, where the arena sat at the top of a wide bank of steps and railings, like a castle perched on top of a rock.

Dozens of people were already walking out, trying to escape the rush of 20,000 concert goers leaving at the same time, flooding the streets of Manchester, trying to get cars out of parking spaces, flag taxis, jump on trams and trains.

The traffic was bumper to bumper. Andrew pulled the car onto the pavement by the steps and phoned Lisa.

It was 10.20pm. She answered straight away.

"Saffie wants to stay for the encore," Lisa said, struggling to make herself heard above the noise inside the arena.

"Ok, I'll find somewhere to park."

"You what?"

"I said: I'll find somewhere to park!"

"Ok. See you in a sec ..."

Andrew drove further along Hunts Back, following the curve of the road into Victoria Station Approach, where more taxis were waiting in a long row.

He found a spot in Cathedral Gardens, just by Manchester Cathedral, where he could keep an eye on the main road. Cars weren't supposed to park in that spot, but it was only for a few minutes. He could move if a traffic warden came along.

He sent Lisa a text to say he had parked and to let him know when they were coming out. There was nothing to do now but wait.

Xander's Nintendo Switch beeped in the background. The car radio was on low volume playing chart music. Children and young teenagers walked along the street with their parents, chattering excitedly, some of them wearing black cat-ear headbands, one of Ariana's trademark fashion accessories, which were being sold by some of the merchandisers around the arena.

Before she was a pop star, Ariana Grande had become

5

famous as a child actor in a children's TV sitcom called Victorious. For that reason, she had always attracted a younger audience, including Saffie.

Andrew kept an eye on the street. He was expecting to see Lisa, Ashlee and Saffie walking along at any moment. He was looking forward to seeing Saffie and hearing about the show. They had bought her the concert tickets for a Christmas present, and she had been counting the days down ever since. Most of the pupils and teachers at Tarleton Primary seemed to know she was attending the concert tonight. She would tell everybody she met about it. "Guess who I'm going to watch ...?"

Andrew checked his watch. 10.30pm. Everything was fine. Everything was normal. His family was fine. His life was normal.

10.31pm. Still sitting in the car, Andrew and Xander heard an almighty bang ring out across Manchester city centre, echoing through the busy streets around the arena building. They felt the vibration of the boom running through their bodies and turned their heads in fear towards the arena, wondering what could have caused such a noise.

Then the screaming started, from around the corner, and out of sight. Young people and their families started running down the street in the opposite direction to the arena, running into one another on the pavement in their hurry to get away from the unknown threat.

Andrew bolted upright, eyes wide open. Xander turned

off his Nintendo Switch. In Xander's lap, Binky's body went rigid and she began growling at the change in atmosphere outside of the car.

Andrew and Xander watched in mute shock as people sprinted past their car. It felt as though their lives had turned into the start of a disaster film, terrifying and unreal at the same time. Andrew could feel his heart beating as adrenaline shot through his veins. This was real and it was unfolding right now, in front of him.

Andrew and Xander didn't know it yet, but a powerful bomb had just exploded outside the Manchester Arena. The person who triggered the bomb had walked straight into the middle of a crowd of young people and their families in the foyer of the arena, intending to kill and maim as many people as he could. It was one of the worst terror attacks ever seen in this country.

But in that moment, in his car with Xander and Binky, all Andrew knew was that a loud bang had caused people on the streets of Manchester to run for their lives. And Lisa, Ashlee and Saffie were nowhere to be seen.

Chapter 2
Bye Bye, Manchester

A few hours earlier

Saffie had been so excited in the thirty-five-minute journey from Leyland into Manchester, smiling and singing songs in the car driven by Ashlee's boyfriend, Craig, a nightclub manager who had offered to drop them off. It was Saffie's first time going out in the big city, and she was about to see her idol live on stage.

"Is this it?" Saffie asked, as they came to a stop on Hunts Bank. "Are we here?"

"This is it," Ashlee said.

Lisa, Ashlee and Saffie stepped onto the pavement, each of them wearing their black cat-ear headbands.

Ashlee kissed Craig goodbye.

"Have a great time," Craig said.

The three of them walked up the long flight of stairs to the entrance into the Manchester Arena. The venue was iconic in the city, where most people called it the MEN arena, despite the sponsorship with the *Manchester Evening News* (MEN) ending in 2011. Many people who live in Manchester will have been to watch a show at the arena or know somebody who has. Some of the biggest names in music have performed there in the past. Rihanna. Whitney Houston. Madonna. Taylor Swift.

It was 6.35pm. Merchandise sellers were flogging posters, T-shirts, and cat-ears on the streets outside, while stewards dressed in hi-vis jackets searched bags for alcohol before letting people through the doors into the bowl-shaped building.

A young man who looked about 18 asked to look inside Lisa's handbag. He had a cursory glance inside before waving them through.

Ashlee went first, leading the three of them through the circular, low ceilinged and brightly lit corridor around the arena as they walked to find their seats. They were at the back in Block 207 on Row A, with a view slightly to the right of the stage. Lisa had chosen a balcony seat so that nobody tall could stand up and block Saffie's line of sight to the stage.

They settled into their seats to watch Victoria Monét, an American pop singer, perform the warm-up act. Saffie hardly paid any attention. All she could talk about was Ariana Grande.

When was she coming? How long until she was on stage?

After Monét had finished, a widescreen projector at the front flashed up with a timer counting down to zero and purple spotlights flashing around the stage.

Saffie was on her feet, clapping her hands and squealing with excitement. She knew that when the timer hit zero, Ariana Grande would make her grand entrance. Thousands of people were shouting and screaming in a frenzy of anticipation.

The timer hit zero, and male dancers in black vest tops appeared, leaping about to the beat of Be Alright, one of Ariana's hit songs. A large screen behind them showed various black and white images of the pop star.

Then, at long last, Ariana Grande herself finally emerged onto the stage. Saffie's screams were lost in a gale of other screams, as Ariana stood at the centre of the stage wearing a black dress and black boots. She started singing her song: Be Alright.

Midnight ... shadows ... when finding love is a battle ...

Lisa could feel the joy in the room. Parents danced and sang along with their children; teenagers had their arms around their friends, taking selfies for their social media accounts.

The concert lasted roughly an hour and a half. Lisa and Ashlee took it in turns to fetch snacks and drinks for Saffie to make sure she didn't miss anything, treats which included a tub of strawberries topped with chocolate and ice cream.

Ariana Grande sang twenty-two songs in total, including Forever Boy, One Last Time and Bang Bang.

At around 10.15pm Ariana started singing Into You.

So baby come light me up,
And maybe I'll let you on it,
A little bit dangerous,
But baby that's how I want it ...

Plumes of smoke hissed into the air on the stage as the show reached its crescendo. Some of the parents and their children were already starting to leave.

Lisa knew it was close to the end, but she also knew that Ariana would probably return to the stage. She was debating whether to leave and escape the crowds or stay and watch the encore. She knew what Saffie wanted to do and it was her night, so the choice was easy.

It was a decision which would stay with Lisa for the rest of her life. What if they had decided to leave early? What if they had got up and walked out of the arena in that moment? How differently their lives might have turned out.

In that moment her phone rang. It was Andrew, who was waiting outside in the car with Xander.

"She's gone off stage, but she's going to come back on for an encore," Lisa said. "I think we're going to stay."

"Of course, no problem. I'll park up and wait," Andrew said.

Ariana walked off the stage, then reappeared minutes later for the encore dressed in black leathers, the stage lighting orange and fiery. Her dancers were gone now. It was just Ariana and the lead guitarist, surrounded by jets of smoke.

She sang Dangerous Woman – slowly, and with feeling, her voice surprisingly powerful for a woman so young and slight.

"Something 'bout you ... makes me feel like a ... dangerous ... woman ..."

She pushed her voice higher and higher, the guitarist keeping up, as she sang her heart out for the finale.

Something 'bout you ...
Something 'bout you ...
Something 'bout you ...
Makes me feel like a dangerous woman ...

The song came to an end. Ariana Grande walked off the stage, kissing and waving to her thousands of adoring fans. "Thank you, Manchester, I love you so much, bye bye ..."

Ashlee, Lisa and Saffie got up to leave, walking from their seats to the outer corridor of the arena, Saffie staying close to her mother in the rush of people. The corridor became a crushing mass of people, pressing to get out. Lisa allowed Ashlee to lead the way. Lisa's sense of direction was not the best. She could get lost in a supermarket, never mind one of Europe's largest concert venues.

Ashlee was walking a few steps ahead. Saffie was next, holding hands with Lisa, dragging her along. "Come on, faster, faster!" Saffie told her mum.

She was excited to see Andrew and Xander. She wanted to tell them everything about the concert.

The three of them walked through a series of doors from the arena building into the City Room, a foyer space where the box office can be found. Across the room on the other side were some more doors which led to a walkway bridge overlooking the platforms of the Manchester Victoria train station. The bridge leads down onto the concourse of the train station itself, where the exits into the street can be found.

The City Room was packed with young people and their families. There were children, parents, grandparents, uncles and aunties, standing and waiting for their loved ones, waiting to pick them up.

People were greeting one another with hugs and kisses, asking about the concert. It was a similar sort of sight to an arrivals hall in an airport, with genuine joy and love in the room.

It was 10.30pm. Ashlee was still a few steps ahead, closer to the walkway than Lisa and Saffie. Saffie was next, holding her mum's hand, chattering excitedly to her mum about the concert. She was so happy.

Lisa never saw the sallow-eyed young man with a patchy beard walking straight at them with a giant rucksack.

He had been hiding at the back of the room in a CCTV blind spot for the best part of an hour. A member of the public had reported him to a security guard for acting suspiciously but nothing had been done.

Now it was too late. He walked out of his hiding spot, down a short flight of stairs, and turned right towards the row of doors into the arena, walking against the tide of people. He put his head down and stepped straight into the middle of a crowd of people.

The time was 10.31pm.

The man reached into the left-hand pocket of his puffer jacket and clicked a trigger button. At that precise moment Lisa and Saffie were five metres away from him.

Some of the survivors who were inside the room described an orange flash followed by an ear-piercing bang, accompanied by the smell of petrol.

The explosion was savage. Lisa was thrown to the floor. After a few seconds – or maybe it was minutes, she would never know which – she opened her eyes. She was lying on her right side, her ears ringing.

A fire alarm was going off but Lisa could not hear it. There was an automated announcement on repeat telling people to evacuate the building. The same message, over, and over, and over. But Lisa didn't hear that either.

The room was full of smoke and dust, and in that fog moved human shapes. Lisa was in shock. Her thoughts were scrambled. She knew it had been a bomb. She knew it was serious. In the shock and confusion, one clear thought emerged.

Saffie. Where was Saffie?

All she could do was move her eyes. She rolled them up and down, and side to side, to try to see if Saffie was anywhere close. She couldn't see her.

She tried to call Saffie's name, but no words came out. She couldn't even manage a croak.

Her breathing felt shallow. She knew she was badly hurt. She felt tired. More tired than she had ever felt in her life. She knew that Saffie was hurt and needed her, just the same as she knew Ashlee had managed to get out of the room. She would never quite understand how she knew those things. She just had a feeling in her stomach that it was true.

She desperately wanted to close her eyes, but she knew that if she closed her eyes she might die, and that would mean leaving Saffie.

Lisa didn't know it, but Saffie was in fact just above her, lying on her back, face up, while Lisa was below her. The pair together formed a rough T shape: Saffie the bar across the top, Lisa the stem, neither of them able to see or hear the other.

They called out for one another, but nobody answered. Their ears were ringing from the blast.

Lisa's body was experiencing severe trauma. She was suffering blood loss and had more than 100 shrapnel wounds from metal nuts and bolts which had been packed into the bomb to cause maximum damage. The nuts and bolts were designed to shred flesh and bone.

Lisa had sustained at least three life-threatening injuries, including a bolt which had entered her chest and lodged itself in the protective sac around her heart. She was losing blood, and it was only a matter of time before her heart went into cardiac arrest.

She was dying and she knew that she was dying. She fought and fought but her resistance to sleep came to an end. She slipped into unconsciousness.

Chapter 3
War Zone

Outside the arena, people were running past Andrew's car, screaming and shouting for help. He was still parked up in Cathedral Gardens, a street away from the arena. He tried to phone Lisa but couldn't get through. He tried Ashlee's phone, but it was the same. It was as if the network had gone down. It was obvious that something terrible had happened.

"Stay here," Andrew said to Xander. He got out of the car and tried to stop a man who was running down the street. "Excuse me ..."

The man didn't stop. He kept on running, eyes bulging, like his brain had been turned to mush by panic.

Some young people ran past. Andrew couldn't stop them, either. Then three middle-aged women paused for breath close to his car. They were in their late forties, with hair worn in bobs.

"Excuse me?" Andrew said, "Do you know what's going on?"

The women shook their heads.

"People are saying maybe a speaker has blown up or a balloon has exploded," said one of them.

"A speaker?" Andrew said doubtfully. It didn't sound anything like a speaker blowing up to him.

"Or maybe … it's a bomb?" said one of the ladies.

A bomb? In Manchester?

Andrew looked along the street, then back at the car, where Xander was staring at him through the windscreen, his big brown eyes alert and anxious.

Should they wait in the car where it was safe? Or should he grab his son and find the rest of the family?

Andrew checked his phone. Still no signal.

Shit.

He had to do something.

He opened the car door. "Let's go find your mum," he told Xander. "Keep hold of Binky."

The two of them walked up Victoria Station Approach, against the tide of people running the other way.

Andrew put his arm around Xander as they reached the corner with Hunts Bank. Andrew's mouth fell open as the view of Hunts Bank opened up in front of them. Put simply it looked like a war zone. Hundreds of people were strewn about the steps and the pavement, many of them bleeding, shouting for help, some of them lying on the ground.

He looked along the pavement. That was when he saw Ashlee, lying there, by Chetham's School of Music.

She was being helped by two young people who were trying to talk to her. Andrew immediately assumed the worst. Ashlee's face and arms were covered in blood, and it looked like she had injuries to her thighs. "Ashlee? Oh, God. Ashlee? Are you ok? Can you hear me?"

Ashlee was not responding.

The two young people – a man and a woman – explained that they were medical students at the local university. They had also been at the concert. "Is she ok?" Andrew said, his heart beating quickly.

"We've checked her over," said the young man, who was slim with short dark hair and a clean-shaven face. He was calm, despite being surrounded by the panic and desperation around him. "She's hurt, but we don't think it's serious."

"Thank God," Andrew said. "What the hell happened?"

"We don't know," the young woman said. She had long blonde hair, and seemed frightened, but was staying with Ashlee, nonetheless. "We think ... maybe it's a bomb."

"A bomb?" Andrew stared at her, hardly able to believe it, yet seeing the evidence around him with his own eyes. "Has she said anything about her mum and sister? Lisa and Saffie? Has she mentioned being with them?"

"No," said the young woman. "I'm sorry."

Ashlee didn't communicate it at that time. But later she would describe what it was like being in the room when the bomb went off. She felt a heat and thought a fire was coming towards her. She crawled out of the room and along the walkway bridge to the train station down below.

Andrew looked along Hunts Bank. It was like a battlefield, littered with injured survivors.

It was 10.50pm.

A police officer was standing outside the train station, about 20 metres away. Andrew and Xander walked up to him.

"That's my daughter," Andrew said, pointing at Ashlee. "My wife and my eight-year-old daughter were with her. I can't find them."

"All I can advise you to do is look around," said the police officer, clearly flustered by the unfolding situation. "There's been an explosion. We're still trying to figure out what happened."

"What about inside the arena?"

"We've got everyone out and are working now to secure it."

Andrew knew he was going to have to find them himself. He started working his way down Hunts Bank, moving from survivor to survivor, conscious he was leading his young son through a street of badly injured children. They walked through puddles of blood as they went from survivor to survivor, looking for Lisa and Saffie.

There were hundreds on the floor. Hundreds more were in hysterics, trying to help. Adults were crying and screaming out in pain.

It was complete chaos.

But what stood out most for Andrew was the screaming of the children. It was a sound he would never forget. It was horrendous: a hellish sound of pure fear from youngsters now involved in something they could not comprehend.

Andrew approached one injured woman to check if it was Lisa. She was surrounded by twenty or thirty people who appeared scared to touch her, not knowing what they were supposed to do. At the same time, they were scared for their own lives and weren't sure whether to simply run away, as many already had, or stay – but for what?

Everyone looked terrified apart from the armed police officers, who had secured the area within minutes.

Andrew kept working his way through the crowds, repeating, "Excuse me, have you seen a young girl? Brown hair, about this high? Excuse me …?"

They reached the bottom of the road. Two armed police officers were blocking the street with plastic railings. They were holding submachine guns, and looked ready to use them.

"Excuse me. I'm looking for my wife and daughter?" Andrew gave them Lisa and Saffie's descriptions.

They had not seen anybody like that, they said, but there were more people gathered on the other side of the arena, in a street called Trinity Way. It was a wider carriageway which runs along the side of the building. Maybe he should try there?

"Ok. Thanks," Andrew said.

Andrew walked to that side of the arena. A crowd of people had gathered, but Lisa and Saffie were nowhere to be seen. Andrew and Xander returned to the armed police officers.

"We can't find them anywhere," Andrew said.

"In that case we'd advise you to go to the hospital," said one of the officers. "Manchester Royal Infirmary is the closest."

Where the hell is that? Andrew thought.

Andrew returned to Ashlee, who by now was propped up against the wall of the music school, but still not making much sense.

The trainee doctors had kept their word and stayed by her side, talking to her, making sure she was as comfortable as she could be given the circumstances.

Andrew didn't want to leave Ashlee, but she was safe, and her condition was stable. He had to find Lisa and Saffie.

"Ash, I've got to go. I've got to find your mum and your sister. These people will take care of you. Craig is on his way, ok?"

They went back to their car in Cathedral Gardens. They got inside and shut the car doors. For the first time, silence.

Andrew knew he was in shock. It almost seemed impossible, and yet, it was real, and happening all around him.

Xander was hardly saying anything. He was sitting quietly, waiting for his dad to make the next move.

Andrew took a moment to steady himself, took a deep breath, then started the engine. "Put your seatbelt on," Andrew said. "We're going to the hospital."

*

Lisa's eyes opened. She hadn't moved. She was still in the City Room, lying on her side, covered in dust.

Why was nobody coming to help? Where were the paramedics or the firefighters?

A police officer appeared at her side. He said something to her that she didn't understand. Her hearing was like white noise.

"Saffie," she managed to say. She was taking shallow, short breaths. She felt like she had been lying there for hours. She felt so, so tired.

Another police officer arrived by her side. "What's your name?"

"Lisa Roussos."

"What's your date of birth, Lisa?"

"September 10th, 48."

Lisa was in a severe state of shock, badly injured, and completely confused. Her age was 48, but her correct date of birth was 10 September, 1968.

It was roughly an hour since the explosion. The fire and rescue service had failed to turn up. Only one paramedic had entered the room in the first forty-five minutes, and only three paramedics in total would ever enter the room, leaving many victims without proper help.

The fire service and ambulance service had decided to hold back until it was safe. The rescue was therefore largely left to a group of Greater Manchester Police (GMP) and British Transport Police (BTP) officers, who were helped by members of the public.

Lisa was losing a dangerous amount of blood. There were no stretchers, so the officers were having to improvise with metal railings and advertising boards.

She was lifted onto a set of metal railings at 11.58pm and

was the second to last person to be moved. The metal bars dug into her injured body, where pieces of shrapnel had lodged in her arms, the back of her legs and back of her torso. The pain was excruciating. Like nothing she had ever experienced before in her life.

A group carried her across the walkway into the train station next door and she was placed on the floor by one of the entrances, where there was a casualty clearing station.

Lisa lay there on that spot until 2.30am – four hours after the bomb had exploded. She was bleeding badly.

"We need to get her to hospital," she heard somebody say, the person's voice sounding urgent.

Lisa continued to drift in and out of consciousness. Time had little meaning by this point. She wanted to die but knew she couldn't. She had to know that Saffie was safe. She felt the sensation of being carried, then heard a helicopter propeller sound.

The next thing she remembered was being on a trolley in a hospital being wheeled quickly down a corridor towards an operating theatre. Doctors were cutting off her jeans and the nurses were removing her jewellery, preparing her for immediate surgery. She just wanted to know Saffie was safe.

Saffie? Where are you?

Please, God. Please, let her be ok.

Please, let her live.

Chapter 4
The Hunt

It was just before midnight. Andrew arrived at Manchester Royal Infirmary, a large teaching hospital located near the city's various university campuses. Ambulances were streaming into the hospital, ferrying survivors from the arena. Off-duty surgeons, doctors and nurses across the city were being contacted by their colleagues, asking them to come in and help with the unprecedented demand caused by more than 1,000 injured survivors.

Andrew parked his car outside the accident and emergency department. He watched as the back doors of the ambulances opened up for the patient inside to be pulled out onto a waiting trolley, then wheeled into the hospital surrounded by the medical teams, sometimes with the families already there, waiting.

He saw one family howling, literally howling, as a survivor was rushed inside, clearly badly injured.

Andrew found two men outside the entrance to the department: a hospital administrator and a police officer. He provided them with a detailed description of Lisa and Saffie. The hospital worker tapped the details into an iPad.

Lisa Roussos. 10/09/1968. White British, blonde, slim build, green eyes, hair down to her shoulders.

Saffie-Rose Roussos. 04/07/2008. White British, straight brown hair, brown eyes, dimples, big cheeks.

The young man finished entering the information. "I'm sorry, but there's nobody here who matches those descriptions."

Andrew's heart sank. He didn't want to leave. What if they were on their way to the hospital in one of the ambulances and he missed them?

"Ok. I'll wait in case they come," he told the man. "That's my car – there." He pointed to the disabled bay 50 yards away, where his Jeep Cherokee was parked. The hospital administrator promised to let him know if they came into the hospital.

Andrew returned to his car, feeling a growing sense of panic. *Why does nobody know where they are?*

Clive Myrie, the BBC anchor, had announced on the rolling news channel that emergency services were dealing with "an incident" at the Manchester Arena. Eyewitnesses had told the BBC they had "heard a loud bang" coming from inside the arena, and footage was playing on a loop showing thousands of people screaming inside the cavernous space of the arena's auditorium. "This all apparently happened at about quarter to eleven this evening at an Ariana Grande pop concert, she was there," Myrie said, "... the pictures that you're seeing there is some footage shot by somebody on their phone of what is clearly panic and hysteria as people are concerned for their safety."

Jan from The Plaice called Andrew on his mobile phone, which was quickly losing battery power.

"Andrew. Oh my God!" Jan said breathlessly. "What's going on?"

"I can't find Lisa or Saffie. I'm frightened to death."

"I'm coming down. I won't be long."

The next call was from Mike, who ran the computer shop on the high street in Leyland and whose daughter, Lily, was Saffie's best friend.

"They're saying on TV some of the kids have been taken to hotels near the arena," Mike said. "And the survivors are in hospitals all around the city."

This was news to Andrew. Saffie could quite easily be in one of those hotels, lost with those other children. Or she might be with Lisa in one of any number of hospitals in Greater Manchester. He could be sitting outside the wrong hospital entirely.

Mike promised to ring around the other hospitals for more information.

Those hours were mental torture for Andrew, who had nothing to do but sit and watch those ambulances arrive, holding his breath as he strained to catch a glimpse of who was being taken out of the back doors and rushed into the hospital. Would the next person be Lisa? Or Saffie?

It was 2am now. Craig called and said he was with Ashlee, who was still propped up on the street corner by the music school, hours after the explosion. "She's alright," Craig reassured Andrew. "We're waiting for an ambulance to pick her up."

Jan arrived at the hospital. She hugged Andrew in the car park and offered him a swig from a cheap bottle of Tesco vodka. Andrew thought about it, but shook his head. He had to stay sharp.

Jan took a long gulp from the bottle to steady her nerves. "I don't believe it," she said. "I just don't believe it. What on earth is the world coming to?"

They sat in the car, hardly speaking, just waiting.

At 4am, Mike called again. Mike may come across as a bit of a joker in his regular daily life, but that night, he was Andrew's saviour. And he had managed to find out some vital information.

"There's a Lisa Roussos in Salford Royal Hospital," he said. "But the date of birth is different. She's down as 10/09/48. They won't give me any more information over the phone."

It had to be her. Their Greek Cypriot surname was unusual, and for the date of birth to be a partial match was too much of a coincidence.

"What about Saffie?" Andrew asked.

"Nothing."

"Shit."

Andrew returned to the young man with the iPad outside the hospital entrance. For four hours he had been sitting outside the wrong hospital, waiting for information about his wife, when all this time she was in Salford Royal Hospital, registered on their system!

"My friend just called to say my wife is in Salford Hospital?" Andrew told him angrily.

"I'm sorry. We can't provide information about Salford Hospital."

Andrew stared at him. "What do you mean you can't provide information about Salford Hospital?"

The young man explained that one hospital could not share information about patients in another hospital. It was against NHS policy.

NHS policy? NHS bloody policy?

Andrew could hardly believe what he was hearing. His wife might be dying in another hospital while he had been sitting in a car park waiting for news that was never going to come. "And what about Saffie?" Andrew demanded. "Where is she?"

"I'm sorry. I don't have those details. There's nothing on our system. I suggest you go to Salford Hospital."

Andrew turned his back and walked away, his blood boiling. What a complete waste of time the last four hours had been. Just when his family needed him most, there he was, parked up in the car park of the wrong bloody hospital.

He got in his car and drove to Salford, Jan in front, Xander in the back, still holding onto Binky, who was looking about in bewilderment with her black eyes. It was a chaotic, frantic, desperate journey. Andrew had to stop to ask people for directions, while Jan searched for a map on her phone.

It was past 4.30am when Andrew arrived at the hospital, about four miles west of Manchester city centre.

He parked in a car park at the back. The whole building looked closed. They knocked on the doors, banged on the windows. Two nurses came and opened up.

"Why is nobody here?" Andrew asked.

"This is the cancer ward," they explained. "It's not open to the public at this time."

Andrew explained what was happening. A bomb had gone off in the city centre, and his wife was somewhere in this hospital. The nurses, both in their forties, and from Manchester themselves, ushered them inside.

They brought them to the hospital's main reception where there were rows of empty seats. One of the nurses left and quickly returned. Two A&E doctors were on the way, she said.

Mike arrived with Tess, his partner, and the five of them sat nervously, waiting for news, each of them looking about, hardly knowing where to look or what to say.

Mike found a number for an emergency service being set up for the families of the victims. Andrew called the number and a woman answered. She asked him for his personal details, along with Saffie's. "The system isn't up and running at the minute," she said, "so I can't tell you the whereabouts of these people. But it won't be long."

It was just another brick wall.

If he couldn't get any information from the emergency hotline, then he would just have to do it himself.

He started calling hotels in the city centre, getting the others to Google the numbers while he made the call. He telephoned a hotel near the arena belonging to one of the larger national chains.

A young man on reception answered. He confirmed they had children at the hotel, who were currently in the guest hotel rooms, where the guests had offered to look after them.

"The children are in ... the guest bedrooms?" Andrew said in astonishment. "You've allowed children to go into rooms on their own with complete strangers?"

"We didn't know what else to do," the young man said, sounding a little panicky. He told Andrew there was nobody at the hotel who appeared to match Saffie's description.

Andrew called another hotel close to the arena. A woman on reception answered and confirmed they also had a number of lost children at the hotel, who were being kept together in the conference room with several members of staff.

At least that was better than going into the guest bedrooms, Andrew thought.

"Have you got a girl called Saffie there?" Andrew said. "She's eight years old with brown hair in a high ponytail, wearing an Ariana Grande T-shirt and a leather jacket?"

"I'm … not sure."

"Can you check?"

The doctors entered the reception. Their faces were grim and serious looking. Something about their faces made Andrew hang up the phone immediately.

"Mr Roussos?" said one of the doctors.

Andrew nodded. "Yes. That's me."

"Ok. Would you mind coming with us?"

Andrew looked at Mike. Mike shrugged. Andrew followed the doctors down a corridor into a private room. In that moment Andrew was utterly convinced they were going to tell him that Lisa was dead. Why else would they want to take him to a room away from the others?

They went into a small side room and sat down in some chairs. The senior doctor, a man in his forties with short brown hair, started explaining to Andrew what had happened to Lisa.

"She's alive," he said, "but she's suffered life-threatening injuries from a bomb explosion. She's got serious damage to her neck, legs and right arm, and needs lots of blood to stabilise her."

She had a number of open wounds on her body caused by flying metal nuts and bolts, the doctor said. She was in a medically induced coma to keep her stable and had been airlifted to Wythenshawe Hospital, which was the leading centre for cardiovascular surgery in Greater Manchester.

It was now a race against time.

Lisa had a break to her left leg which was life-threatening. The blood had been cut off entirely in the lower part of her left leg, which could lead to amputation or death if the surgeons couldn't repair it quickly. She had been flown by helicopter to Wythenshawe for emergency surgery.

"You should prepare yourself for the worst, Mr Roussos," said one of the doctors, quietly. "But the best thing you can do right now … is get to Wythenshawe Hospital."

Chapter 5
A Centimetre from Death

Andrew sat in the room with the two doctors, stunned and trying to hold it together. Ashlee was hurt on her way to one hospital, Saffie was missing, and now he was expected to drive to another hospital twelve miles away where surgeons were battling to save Lisa's life.

A few hours ago he had been locking up the shop, looking forward to seeing them after a pop concert.

He walked back to the hospital reception in a daze. He practically floated his way there. He stood in front of the group, hardly knowing what to say. Then he told them.

Jan was in pieces. Xander was a blank page, stunned, hardly able to believe what was happening. Mike had his head in his hands.

Andrew knew they had to get to Wythenshawe Hospital, but he felt certain that Saffie was lost somewhere in the city centre, looking for him and Lisa. She was probably in one of those hotels. What if she was in a guest bedroom with a complete stranger?

Mike promised to search for Saffie and take Binky with him. "Thanks Mike," Andrew said.

Andrew, Jan and Xander set off on another journey in the early hours of the morning, driving through Salford, then into south Manchester towards the outskirts of Cheshire.

It was 6.30am on Tuesday morning when they arrived in Wythenshawe Hospital car park.

Andrew was running on empty, kept going through a mixture of fear and adrenaline.

He gave his details to the hospital reception, and Daniella, the ward manager from the intensive care unit (ICU), came down to meet him. Daniella was a German lady with short blonde hair and an air of authority. She ran one of the most pressured wards in the hospital, and that came with big responsibilities, which she carried on broad shoulders.

She confirmed that Lisa had been flown in by helicopter in an induced coma.

The purpose of the induced coma was to keep her still and stable because of the amount of shrapnel in her body and blood loss, Daniella explained.

Lisa had been given paralysing agents which had been infused into her bloodstream via a cannula in her hand, and had a machine to help her breathe during the flight to the hospital.

Andrew was tired and emotional. But he knew how important it was to stay alert and focused. There would be family and friends relying on him for the right information. And that meant absorbing as much of the medical detail as he could.

Lisa's surgeon arrived at reception. Mark Welch was a vascular surgeon in his late fifties, with curly white hair and bushy white eyebrows. He was one of the best vascular surgeons in the country, a type of surgeon who specialises in repairing blood vessels.

Welch was famous amongst theatre nurses in the hospital for conducting operations to the sound of Meat Loaf and Led Zeppelin. At one stage he was the secretary for the Deep Purple fan club.

"Lisa is alive," Welch said. "But she has serious injuries, as you know, and she has lost a lot of blood."

The blood flow into her left lower leg was blocked, which risked leading to amputation of leg, or even death. Welch's team had fought through the early hours to free that blockage, and he had made a life-changing decision for Lisa. He had decided to try to save her leg.

The surgery had started at 1.30am and lasted for six hours. The surgeons knew they had four hours from the point where the blood supply was cut off in order to save her leg. Anything after that would mean Lisa would have to lose it.

The explosion happened at 10.31pm – giving them sixty minutes to complete the surgery and check the blood flow.

Welch put a silicon tube between the two ends of the severed artery to allow blood to flow through and essentially give her lower leg a drink. The procedure bought the team a little more time.

Welch decided to take a vein from Lisa's right leg which he would try to insert into her left leg to repair the damaged artery. Some of the theatre nurses present had never seen such a procedure before, and many at the hospital still talk about Welch's work under pressure to this very day.

Welch took a breath and made a cut over the vein and physically dissected it. Blood only flows one way through a vein. Welch turned it upside down to make it work in her other leg: a delicate procedure known as a reverse vein graft.

He used a small clamp to hold the vein in place in the damaged artery, then used a fine suture to put a number of stiches around the circumference of the vein.

So far, so good.

They would only know for certain it had worked when they let the clamps off. Then they would see if her leg filled with blood, or if the graft had worked and allowed blood to flow from the top of her leg into the bottom of her leg.

"Clamps off," Welch ordered the team.

The team removed the clamps. They held their collective breath as they peered into Lisa's open leg wound. Would the vein leak, or would it work? Welch knew if the leg filled with blood, he would have no choice but to resort to Plan B, which meant amputation.

Come on.

The operation worked. The graft had mended the artery, and Lisa's leg was getting the blood it needed without any leaking.

It was a remarkable piece of precision surgery in the early hours of the morning. And it had most likely saved Lisa's life – for now. Scans had since revealed she had two more life-threatening injuries. The first was a metal nut in her heart sac, the protective layer around the heart. The shrapnel was precisely one centimetre away from the heart itself. If the nut had penetrated, then she would most likely be dead. She had come within ten millimetres of being killed by the arena bomb blast.

There was also a metal nut lodged in the back of her neck – her second cervical vertebra, to be exact – pushing against one of her nerves, putting her at risk of paralysis from the neck down. The injury was also considered life-threatening due to its position so high in the neck.

Then there were her other injuries: not quite so life-threatening, but dangerous because of their cumulative effect on the body. The human body can only take so much before it shuts down.

Lisa had fractures to her right forearm, and an injury to her right hand with bone loss to her fingers and loss of her median nerve, which helps move the forearm, wrist, hand and fingers. The doctors knew that if she survived then her right hand would need to be completely reconstructed.

She had fractures to both femurs, the longest, strongest bone in the body, found in the thigh. She had multiple fractures to her spine. She had shrapnel in her chest and limbs, as well as a wound to her right cheek and right ear, which had damaged Lisa's eardrum. In total she had more than 100 injuries to her body.

Welch said she was being kept in a medically induced coma. A ventilator machine was helping her breathe and it was uncertain whether or not she would be able to breathe on her own, given the extent of her injuries.

Andrew listened carefully to the surgeons, doing his best

to remember what they were saying. It felt like a tidal wave of information. He was doing his best to hold it together, but there was one question he needed to know the answer to. "Is she going to make it?" Andrew said.

The surgeons looked at one another. Then they broke it to him. Her chances of survival were around fifteen per cent. If she did survive, there was a ninety per cent chance she would be paralysed from the neck down because of the bolt in her neck. The next 24 hours were crucial.

"I'm sorry," Welch said, walking away.

Fifteen per cent.

It was as if Andrew's worst nightmare was unfolding right in front of him. How could this be happening?

Andrew turned to Daniella, the ICU ward manager. His wife was fighting for her life. But at least he had found her. Now he needed to find Saffie.

"Daniella, please. I need to find my daughter, Saffie. She was with Lisa when the bomb went off. We don't know where she is. Is there anything you can do?"

Daniella nodded. "I think I know somebody who can help," she said.

She left the reception area and came back after a few minutes with a giant of a man, six feet four inches, and bald-headed. Russ, a detective for Greater Manchester Police, looked like he could have been a professional wrestler in another life. He introduced himself and explained that he had been posted to the hospital to look after the bomb survivors and their families.

Daniella explained the problem. Saffie was missing.

"Russ. Please. My wife is lying in ICU, on death's door. I need to find my daughter. She's eight years old. She's lost somewhere in Manchester. Can you help me?" Andrew asked.

Russ was a family man himself with his own wife and kids. "Do you have a photograph?" he said.

Andrew gave him one of Saffie on a family trip to New York, sitting by a window in the hotel, hair plaited to one side, the Empire State Building lit up pink on the skyline behind her.

"Ok. Sit tight," Russ said. "I'll come back with some answers. I promise."

He left the hospital and went into Manchester to find Saffie.

By now the country was waking up to learn the full scale of the terror atrocity in the city, one of the worst attacks ever seen in the UK, where children and young people had clearly been targeted with their families by a person or persons unknown.

This was international news. Of course, none of that mattered to Andrew. He just wanted to know his daughter was safe.

Andrew felt reassured Russ was on the case. At least somebody in authority was now trying to find her. There was something about Russ that made Andrew think he would come good on his promise. It also gave him the headspace to think about what had to come next.

Andrew walked behind Daniella through the hospital corridors to the intensive care unit, knowing it was time to face the awful truth about what had happened to Lisa.

*

The ICU was subject to a high level of security and needed a nurse or doctor to buzz people inside. The ward had previously admitted members of the city's drug gangs who had been stabbed or shot by rival criminals and it had to have tight security in case their assassins arrived at the hospital in order to finish the job. There were also precautions in place due to the attentions of the media in high profile cases.

Daniella and Andrew were buzzed into the secure unit. Straight through the doors was a waiting room for relatives, and a corridor with small private rooms where patients could get updates from doctors and nurses about their loved ones.

The ward was in the shape of an L. Straight down the corridor from the waiting area was a nurses' station, which then branched off into a row of beds. Beside the station was bed number nine, where nurses placed the most critical patient on the ward. This was due to convenience, since it made sense to have the bed where they would be working most frequently next to their station.

Andrew turned the corner and saw bed number nine. Inside the bed was Lisa. Or rather, what the nurses said was Lisa.

He took a sharp intake of air. The blood drained out of his face, and his heart raced.

My God.

Lisa's eyes were closed. She was propped up in the bed and bandaged from head to toe. In fact, the only part of her body free from bandages was her face. Her features were so bruised and swollen that it didn't even look like Lisa. She looked like she had put on about ten stone in weight.

She had two tubes going up her nose, and three tubes going into her mouth. She was hooked up to a ventilator, and beside her was an observations monitor measuring her heart rate, the oxygen levels in her blood, blood pressure, carbon dioxide levels, and temperature.

Andrew broke down in tears. It was too awful to comprehend. How could this happen to his beautiful wife?

"I don't know what to do," Andrew said, feeling utterly lost in that moment.

"Be strong," Daniella said.

He had never been around somebody badly sick or hurt before. Most of his close relatives remained alive and well. He found it difficult to know how to act.

The nurses encouraged him to hold Lisa's hand and talk to her. "The hearing is the last to go. She might be able to hear you," they told him.

Andrew sat in the chair by her bed, took hold of her limp hand, and tried to think of something to say, watching the mechanical ventilator pump air in and out of Lisa's lungs, keeping her alive.

The machine made a woosh, woosh noise as the air was forced in and out of her body.

If that machine was keeping her alive, did that mean, in fact, she was dead?

That was the kind of thought that went through Andrew's mind as he tried to compose himself before he tried to say the right words.

What was he supposed to say? Did he tell her the truth? That Ashlee had been badly hurt, Saffie was missing, and she had a 15 per cent chance of survival? How could he tell her that?

Or did he tell her everything was going to be ok? That seemed so false. So fake.

"I'm sorry," he told the nurses. "I'm sorry. I just can't."

Andrew stood up from the chair and walked away from Lisa's bed, that *woosh woosh* sound in his ears as he turned the corner by the nurse's station and left the unit, knowing that their lives were never going to be the same again.

Chapter 6
Russ Returns

Xander was in the coffee shop with Jan, waiting for news. Andrew returned from Lisa's ward and sat down with them.

"How's mum?" Xander said anxiously.

Andrew steadied himself. Then did his best to explain in words that Xander could understand. "She's badly injured. They've put her in a coma, like a sleep, so her body can heal itself better."

"Can I see her?"

"I don't think that's a good idea, mate," he said. "Not right now. She doesn't look like mummy."

Xander's face went white. He didn't ask again. He didn't even cry. He had hardly said two words since walking through those streets full of injured people at the arena.

It was now 10.30am. Andrew was receiving phone calls and messages from their friends and family, begging for an update on Lisa, Ashlee and Saffie. Everybody knew they had been at the concert, and word was getting around.

Lisa was hurt and Saffie was still missing.

Stephen, Lisa's brother, had called to say he was on his way to the hospital. He owned his own business in Nottingham, building public address systems for stadiums. He had dropped everything to head to Wythenshawe Hospital.

43

Sam, one of Lisa's oldest and dearest friends from Nottingham, had also called Andrew, asking for news about Lisa. "Is this real?" she kept saying, her voice upset on the phone. "Is this real, Andrew?"

Andrew told her the truth, straight. Lisa was on life support in the intensive care unit. It was touch and go.

Sam got a flight back from her holiday the very next day. She wanted to visit Lisa and be around the hospital to do anything she could to support the family. Dawn, another of Lisa's closest friends, also made her way straight to the hospital.

Andrew held off speaking to his father, Tony, in Cyprus. He would want to know about Saffie, his granddaughter, who he called "the baby". Andrew didn't want to speak to him until he could give him a definitive answer.

By now Mike had tried most of the hotels around the arena in the city centre asking for Saffie. Nobody had seen her. Russ had disappeared into Manchester and not come back yet.

That morning was agonising. In Andrew's mind, Saffie was out there, somewhere alone, lost and afraid, looking for her mother and father.

At around midday, Andrew, sitting at a table in the Costa coffee shop by the main entrance, watched Russ walk into the hospital and head straight towards one of the nurses inside. Andrew watched him carefully.

Why had Russ gone to the nurse first, rather than come and find him?

In those moments, tiny little details can stay with you for the rest of your life. People can instinctively feel when something is not ok from watching another person's body language and almost subconsciously reading the signals.

Andrew had a bad feeling about the way Russ was speaking to the nurse in the corridor. There was just something about his demeanour. He looked *heavy*.

Russ spoke with the nurse for a few minutes, then walked into the coffee shop and approached Andrew's table.

"Andrew, can I have you for a moment? We're just organising a room."

Andrew stood up. Why couldn't he just tell him about Saffie? Why couldn't he just say she was safe? That she was in a hotel or police station in Manchester city centre? Why did they need a room?

Xander and Jan stayed in the coffee shop, while Andrew followed the detective down a hospital corridor. They were shown into a private consultation room in the cardiology department. Two more detectives joined them. They sat down around a table. Nobody said anything.

Andrew looked at Russ.

It was like Russ had something to say but didn't want to say it. He didn't want to say the words.

Then he did.

"Saffie didn't make it."

The room was silent. Nobody said a word. Not a single word.

Andrew stared at Russ. "What?"

"She didn't make it. I'm sorry."

Andrew felt like he was in a dream. At some point he would realise that none of this was real and wake up from this living nightmare in his bedroom above the shop in Leyland.

What he was being told was simply impossible. There was no way Saffie could be dead.

How could she be dead?

"I'm so sorry," Russ said.

The other detectives mumbled the same. Big men with broad shoulders. All fathers themselves. Wet-eyed and devastated. They sat there, the four men, around the table in that little room in the hospital, hardly knowing where to look.

Andrew had convinced himself that she was lost in the city centre, doing cartwheels in a hotel conference room full of children, entertaining the hotel staff with her antics.

Not for one moment had he contemplated the possibility that she might have been killed by the blast. Perhaps because his brain wouldn't allow him to go there. He felt numb. He was in shock.

"What am I going to tell Xander?"

"Tell him straight," Russ said. "It's the only thing you can do."

Andrew left the room and walked back to the coffee shop. He was in a daze. He could see himself walking along the corridor. It was like he was watching himself in an outer body experience.

He found Xander and told him to come to the room. Xander followed his father, unquestioningly. They entered the room and sat down at the table. Russ broke the news to Xander. "Saffie didn't make it, son. I'm sorry."

Xander looked up at his father. He was confused. He had never heard that phrase before: *didn't make it.* "What does he mean?"

"She just ... she didn't make it, mate."

Xander looked at each of their faces. Then he understood what he was being told. His sister had died in the explosion at the arena. The same one which had hurt his mum.

Xander sat on Andrew's knee and put his head on his father's chest. "What do we do now?" Xander said.

"I don't know," Andrew said.

The three detectives remained in their seats, heads bowed, as if in prayer.

Saffie didn't make it. She was gone.

47

Chapter 7
The Fight for Life

It was the day after the arena bomb. The UK government was trying to cope with news of its most deadly terror attack since the London bombings of 7 July, 2005. Armed troops were deployed to guard key locations across the country, including Buckingham Palace, Downing Street, the Palace of Westminster and foreign embassies.

The Prime Minister, Theresa May, had been informed during an emergency meeting that the country's threat level had been raised to "critical", which meant that another terrorist attack was highly likely in the near future.

Politicians from around the world were sending messages of support to Manchester and the UK. US President Donald Trump, who was in Bethlehem, where he was meeting Palestinian President Mahmoud Abbas, condemned the "murder of so many young, beautiful, innocent people" and said the "wicked ideology" of the "evil losers" responsible would be "completely obliterated".

The Chinese President, Xi Jinping, sent a message to Queen Elizabeth II expressing his sincere condolences to those killed and injured. "The Chinese people are firmly standing together with the British people at this difficult time," Xi said.

German chancellor Angela Merkel said, "I assure the people in Britain: Germany stands by your side."

While Japan's Prime Minister Shinzo Abe said: "On behalf of the government of Japan and the Japanese people, I would like to express my heartfelt condolences to the victims and extend our sympathies to those who have been injured."

Among the first to be named as those who had lost their lives were John Atkinson, 28, from Bury in Greater Manchester; Georgina Callander, 18, from Tarleton in Lancashire; and Saffie-Rose Roussos, aged eight, the youngest victim of the attack, which had claimed 22 lives and left more than 1,000 people injured.

Islamic State, a jihadist group with bases in the Middle East and Africa, was quick to announce it was behind the attack, but this could not be verified.

Was the arena bomb part of a wider attack on the UK? Was the bomber working with others poised to carry out further atrocities on innocent members of the public?

The Prime Minister and Home Secretary wanted the answers to those questions. And quickly.

*

Back at Wythenshawe hospital, Andrew was struggling to cope with the number of telephone calls he was receiving from friends and relatives. His father, Tony, and mother, Helen, now separated, had been calling him from Cyprus since the bomb.

Andrew knew he couldn't put off speaking to them any longer: not now he knew the truth about Saffie.

Andrew called his dad.

Tony answered, sounding breathless. "Son? What's going on? What's happened?"

Andrew explained. A bomb had gone off in Manchester after the pop concert. Ashlee was hurt. Lisa was critical in hospital.

Tony took a sharp intake of breath. It was hard for him to take it in. He led a quiet life in Cyprus, these days. Every day was the same, slow and sunny and dreamy. The idea his family had been caught up in a terror attack was beyond belief.

"What about the baby?" Tony said, meaning Saffie, his beloved granddaughter.

Andrew paused. This was one of the moments he had been dreading. It was all he could do to say the words. "She didn't make it, dad."

"What do you mean?"

"I mean she didn't make it. She died."

Tony was a macho, alpha male type of a father. He was from a long line of fathers who believed showing emotion to your children was a sign of weakness. It was important to remain strong at all times, especially in times of crisis. "I'm coming over," Tony said gruffly.

Andrew knew there was no point in refusing. His father would do what he pleased, no matter what he said. Tony may have been in his late seventies, but he had the energy of a man half his age.

Andrew spoke to Chris, his brother, then Helen, his

mother, then all the various aunties and uncles, and Lisa's friends.

Each time he had to tell them the same story, over and over again. Saffie had been caught up in the terror attack at the Ariana Grande pop concert. She had died.

The hospital had offered Andrew a psychiatrist, but he refused. It wasn't the right time. There was nothing a psychiatrist could do or say to make him feel any better. This was about survival. Pure and simple. It was about keeping the family together as best he could and focusing on Lisa pulling through.

Grief could come later.

That afternoon, Andrew and Xander drove to Bolton Hospital to visit Ashlee. She was recovering from her own surgery to remove pieces of shrapnel from her body.

Ashlee was in shock, like the rest of them. She had already heard the news about Saffie. By now it was all over the TV and the radio. She hugged Andrew and cried. They exchanged few words. What could anybody say? Nobody could bring her back.

On the way out of the hospital Andrew bumped into Ashlee's father, Lisa's first husband, who, coincidentally, was also called Andrew. They had maintained a good relationship over the years regarding Ashlee.

He had been a good father to Ashlee. And he was clearly devastated about Saffie.

"If there's anything you need, mate?" he said.

Andrew nodded, and carried on walking down the

hospital corridor, Xander walking beside him. They were exhausted. It was Tuesday afternoon and they had still not slept.

They decided to head back to Leyland. Andrew thought it might be a good idea to get a few hours' sleep in the apartment. They could use the time to pick up some essentials for the hospital. Fresh clothes. New underwear. Toothbrushes and toothpaste.

They arrived at Hough Lane to find it besieged by TV vans, TV cameras, and news reporters. Saffie had been one of the first people to be named as a victim of the arena bomb. Her photogenic looks combined with her young age was going to make the family a focal point for the media.

The reporters were looking for an update on Lisa's condition. They had been speaking to local shopkeepers and customers on the high street, getting reaction to the news about the Roussos family being caught up in the attack.

Andrew decided it wasn't the right moment to speak. He pulled the car into a side street to avoid being seen. Martin, whose wife, Karen, ran a furniture shop two doors up, came out to help.

"Andrew. I'm so sorry. I just can't believe it. I'll help you into the apartment."

A sharp-eyed TV reporter saw them and approached. "Mr Roussos? I'm sorry to bother you at a time like this. How is Lisa doing? Can you say anything about her condition?"

"He doesn't want to talk to anybody right now," Martin said.

"I'll speak later. Is that ok?" Andrew said.

Andrew opened the side door into the shop. He took Xander and they went upstairs to the apartment.

Xander walked into his parents' bedroom and lay down on the bed, curling up on his side, not saying a word. He shut his eyes.

Andrew was about to walk into the room and lie down next to Xander when he caught a glimpse of Saffie's bedroom through the open doorway.

He paused a moment and looked inside.

Saffie's vest tops were strewn across the floor where she had thrown them, probably in a rush to try out different outfits; a drawer from a chest of drawers was half-pulled out; her bed was unmade from the night before. It was almost as if she had just run out the door and would be back in a few minutes. There was something so raw and immediate and *normal* about that scene.

A feeling of black dread settled onto Andrew's shoulders, like nothing he had ever experienced.

He imagined Saffie in the apartment, shouting him from the kitchen, asking for food to feed her endless appetite; bouncing on the sofa; filming Xander with her phone just to annoy him; hiding yoghurt pots in Xander's school shoes; jumping out of cardboard boxes at Chrissy; laughing and dancing and joking.

How could she be gone?

He walked into his bedroom and lay down on the double bed beside Xander. He tried to close his eyes, but he ended

53

up lying on his back, staring up at the ceiling. They had been so happy.

There was something eerie about the apartment now. It felt so quiet and empty.

"Shall we go back to the hospital?" Andrew said.

"Ok, dad," Xander said.

They gathered some essentials and headed back in the car. The hospital management had arranged for them to have their own private bedroom on the cancer ward. It had two single beds and a bathroom with a shower. Anything was better than the apartment, Andrew thought.

Andrew settled Xander into the room and returned to ICU to check on Lisa's progress. She was being looked after by some of the most experienced and skilled nurses in the hospital trust, including Kate, Simon, David, Lorraine, Jo and Sue.

Andrew grew particularly close to Lorraine, a mother of three, who had a great deal of empathy for her patients. Andrew could tell this was more than a job to Lorraine. She was one of life's givers, and nursing was a perfect career choice for her.

That evening, Andrew visited Lisa. He stood over her bed, listening to the beeping machines and monitors, watching that damned ventilator machine pushing her stomach up and down.

Andrew watched Lisa. Her head bandaged. Her faced bruised.

His beautiful wife, who had taught him how to live again after his disastrous first marriage. The mother of his children. He noticed Lorraine standing next to him.

"I don't know what to say," Andrew said quietly.

"Just let her hear your voice," she said gently.

"Do you think it will help?"

"Yes. I do."

Andrew moved from the bottom of the bed to the chair beside her. He took her hand in his hand.

"Lisa. It's me. Andrew. You've been hurt in an explosion at the concert. You're in a hospital now with the nurses and the doctors. I'm here. And I'm never going to leave. I love you ..."

He had lost Saffie. He couldn't lose Lisa, too. He closed his eyes, and prayed for a miracle.

Chapter 8
A Nation's Prayers

Somebody was knocking on the door of their room.

Andrew opened his eyes. He checked the clock.

3am. Who was knocking on the door at 3am? He only got to sleep four hours ago. In Andrew's mind, that could only mean one thing. Lisa had died in the night. Why else would somebody be knocking on the door at such a time?

Xander was asleep next to him. In the other bed was Tony, his father, who had arrived from Cyprus on a British Airways flight, provided free of charge by the airline.

Andrew got out of bed and opened the door in his pyjamas to find a nurse standing in the corridor.

"I'm sorry, Mr Roussos," she said, "but there's two police officers who would like to speak with you urgently."

"What, right now?"

The nurse nodded.

Andrew dressed himself and left the room. The nurse took him to a room where two police officers were waiting.

He sat down. His heart was thumping.

Lisa's dead. She's dead.

"We wanted to be the first to let you know," said one of them, "so that you have fair warning and it doesn't come as too much of a shock ... Saffie's photograph is going to be on the front pages of the newspapers tomorrow."

Andrew blinked in confusion. "Is that it? Is that why you woke me in the middle of the night?"

They nodded.

Andrew shook his head in frustration. He walked out of the room and went back to his room on the cancer ward.

Why did they wake him up to tell him that? This story was international news. Of course Saffie was going to be on the front page. She was the youngest victim!

He got back into bed but couldn't sleep. He found himself scrolling through videos of Saffie at the concert. She was so beautiful. Her full cheeks, clear complexion, big brown eyes streaked with amber. He remembered how old ladies would stop her in the street to comment, she was so beautiful.

She looked so happy in those videos.

At about 8am Andrew gave up trying to sleep. He headed to the ICU to see Lisa. On his way was a WHSmith with a newspaper rack outside.

The police officers had been right, at least. Pretty much every newspaper had a photograph of Saffie on the front. Most of them had used a picture of her in the back of Craig's car on the way to the concert, a big grin on her face.

Andrew pressed the door buzzer into the unit. "Password, please?" said a nurse.

"Binky."

The nurse buzzed him inside.

He arrived by Lisa's bed to find a number of surgeons, doctors and nurses having a meeting.

The plan was to carry out as many procedures as possible in each surgery. That way they could minimise the amount of time she was in theatre and maximise her recovery time.

Andrew met two plastic surgeons who would be taking the lead in many of Lisa's future operations.

Jonathan Duncan was a young Scottish surgeon with a handsome face and a comforting bedside manner. He was known for his excellent communication skills with patients. For the past few years he had been rebuilding the hospital's breast reconstruction service, making it a centre of excellence in the region.

Duncan would be working alongside his mentor, Professor Vivien Lees, one of the country's leading plastic and hand surgeons. She was going to attempt to rebuild Lisa's damaged right hand as best she could. Andrew found her to be kind, warm and considerate; while Professor Lees found Andrew to be a strong figure in his family, who had not allowed his recent bereavement to swallow him up.

The hospital was in crisis mode. More than 100 survivors had been taken there. Many of them needed multiple and complex surgeries.

The surgeons set up three separate operating theatres to cope with the workload, with three separate teams.

The rooms ran around the clock for the first 72 hours, dealing with children, young people and their relatives who had been hurt by flying nuts and bolts packed into the bomb. Many of the survivors had to be given blood tests since some of the shrapnel had passed through several bodies first before getting lodged. Fortunately, there were no issues with blood infections on that front.

Lisa's injuries were almost unprecedented for the hospital. They were similar to those of a soldier who had stepped on an improvised explosive device. It was effectively a war injury.

As part of a military operation there would typically be a field hospital geared up to treat her type of injuries. But Lisa was in a civilian hospital, where the doctors had to think on their feet.

She had been through another operation since arriving. Surgeons had used a pair of tweezers to remove a metal nut about the size of a polo mint lodged in her pericardium, a fluid-filled sac which surrounds and protects the heart. The operation was a success.

But she still had 126 pieces of nuts and bolts embedded in her body, most of them the size of a polo mint. The backs of her legs, in particular behind her knees, were the worst affected. The hospital had invited British Army medics to speak to their staff in order to advise the best way forward with the operations.

The army doctors advised Professor Lees to be aggressive in removing the dead tissue around the shrapnel in order to prevent infection. If bacteria got into the dead tissue it could become infected and lead to sepsis, a form of blood poisoning. This could be lethal.

Debridement, which means the cutting away of dead

tissue, was the number one method of getting rid of infection, along with a course of strong antibiotics.

Professor Lees and Jonathan Duncan explained to Andrew what would happen next. Lisa would need skin grafts, where healthy skin was taken from Lisa's body and used in places where she had damaged skin, such as her body and the backs of her legs.

In simple terms, the dead tissue would be "debrided", or cut away, which would leave a hole, then skin grafts would be put over the hole to heal and close the wounds, reducing the risk of infection.

"Will she be able to walk?" Andrew asked.

"We're not sure about paralysis at this stage," said Professor Lees, who had short brown hair and a fringe, kindly eyes, and a warm smile. There was something about her maternal manner which meant people would immediately trust her. "We've seen Lisa's legs move but we're not sure about one of her arms. It might mean her arm is paralysed. And she'll need a lot of work on her hand and wrist over a period of time, as well as the other wounds."

Professor Lees said she would be operating on the nut found at the back of Lisa's neck, which was creating a risk of paralysis, or even death. "I'll be doing that alongside a neurosurgeon on Friday," she said. "We will know more after that."

*

Friday lunchtime Lisa was wheeled in her ICU bed down the corridor straight into the operating theatre. Critical patients like Lisa would remain in their beds the entire time. There was no point trying to lift her out onto a trolley and into another bed for the operation. Much better for her to remain in one bed.

Andrew was given permission to walk alongside her as they wheeled her into a small private room outside the operating theatre, known as the anaesthetic room. Usually it was a place where only the mothers and fathers of young children were allowed access. The nurses found that some children could get nervous about being put to sleep for an operation, so being with their parents could be an important way to help them relax.

A special exception had been made for Andrew, given what he was going through.

Andrew watched as the theatre doors opened and Lisa was wheeled into the operating theatre, where Professor Lees stood in the centre of the room in her blue scrubs, blue face mask, and blue theatre hat. The only thing visible were her kindly eyes.

The theatre team lifted Lisa up and turned her onto her front so that Professor Lees and the neurosurgeon, Mr van Popta, could operate.

The nut in Lisa's neck was pushing down on an important nerve in her second cervical vertebra, high up and close to her spine. It could cause damage to her central nervous system.

Mr van Popta used a pair of metal grasping forceps to tease it out. Professor Lees assisted him in doing so, retracting the tissue back to give van Popta the best possible view and a clean visible field. Mr van Popta managed to get the nut out on the first attempt.

Professor Lees gave an internal sigh of relief. She didn't show it – she was used to working under such immense pressure – but that was by far the most delicate part of the operation. The success of removing that metal nut out of Lisa's neck would be the difference to whether she lived or died, or walked or remained paralysed from the neck down for the rest of her life.

Now the nut was removed, the surgeons turned their attentions to the shrapnel in the backs of her legs, taking out the nuts and bolts piece by piece, putting them into a metal tray on the side. Some of it was given to the police forensic teams for evidence.

Professor Lees had been working around the clock since the bomb had detonated. The hospital was under pressure. Not just the surgeons, but the teams which wrapped around them, providing them with the right equipment, like dressings and swabs and sterilised tools.

They were running out of dressings and bandages. The hospital staff were having to put pressure on their procurement and supply chains to get the equipment it needed to continue the round-the-clock operations on the survivors.

The team rotated Lisa back so she was lying face up so

that Professor Lees could attach a fixator to her right hand. Some of her fingers were floppy due to being fractured and broken. A piece of shrapnel from the bomb had passed right through the middle of her hand.

Professor Lees would have to rebuild her right hand – which was Lisa's dominant hand – and replace those bones.

She attached the fixator and put screws in several places around her hand with a bar across it in order to hold the whole thing in place. This would help keep her hand safe from being injured further.

Outside, Andrew was pacing the corridors of the hospital. He had been assigned a new police liaison officer. Des was a smartly dressed police officer in his forties, who had a cheerful demeanour. Andrew and Des clicked immediately. Des was the sort of person Andrew could see himself being friends with in more normal circumstances. Des had been in the police for thirty years, and clearly knew what he was talking about.

He had a natural empathy for dealing with the victims of crime and their families, and an easy-going personality, which made him a perfect fit for the work of a family liaison.

There was nothing to do that Friday afternoon except wait. Des thought it might do Andrew good to get out of the hospital and get some air. He suggested going to St Ann's Square in Manchester, where people had been leaving tributes for the victims of the Manchester Arena attack.

Andrew agreed. Des drove him down, taking Xander and Andrew's father, Tony, along for the ride. When they arrived in the square, right at the heart of the shopping district in Manchester city centre, Andrew could hardly believe it.

The square had become a carpet of flowers, pink balloons, candles, and sympathy cards. There were thousands upon thousands of bouquets with teddy bears resting on top. The names of some of those who died were written on cards.

Andrew bent down to read some of the cards left for Saffie.

RIP Saffie my darling. God's most beautiful angel, read one, left by a complete stranger.

A policewoman on duty in the square recognised Andrew and came straight over. She hugged him. She had three daughters herself. She asked about Lisa. "I'm so sorry," she said, tears in her eyes.

Andrew found the experience emotional but uplifting. All these people who cared about what had happened to Saffie. They got back to the hospital where Daniella was waiting for them.

She took them behind the reception desk where there was a growing pile of shopping bags. They were presents from members of the public meant for Andrew.

Andrew was now the proud owner of thirty-four toothbrushes and more than a hundred tubes of toothpaste, along with enough fruit to open up his own greengrocer's. It was the same back at the shop in Leyland. People were turning up with wads of cash in envelopes.

Andrew felt overwhelmed with gratitude. And for the first time since the bomb had gone off, he didn't feel quite so alone.

*

In the late afternoon, Andrew's phone rang. The call came from an unknown number.

"Andrew Roussos?"

"Yes."

"Hello. I'm the neurosurgeon who carried out the operation on Lisa. I'm travelling down to London today. But I just wanted to call you and let you know ... Lisa's operation was a complete success. Everything should be fine."

Andrew breathed a deep sigh of relief. "I don't know what to say," he said. "Thank you."

"Not a problem. I wish you and your family all the best. Our hearts are with you."

Chapter 9
Limbo is a White Room

Life for Andrew and Xander quickly became a routine of waking up in the morning, and Tony taking Xander while Andrew went to check on Lisa.

Andrew kept Xander away from the intensive care unit, thinking it would be too much to see his mother in such a state, surrounded by the life and death situations on the ward. It was terrifying and strange to see people in their beds being brought back to life with electric shocks. Andrew was amazed one morning when Lorraine resuscitated a patient with chest compressions, only to appear a few minutes later as if nothing unusual had happened. "Cup of tea and a biscuit?" she said.

He blinked at her. *Who are these people?*

Life and death seemed like part of their routine. And after a while, seeing people in those states became normal even for Andrew.

Opposite Lisa's bed was a middle-aged couple who were also caught up in the attack – a mother and a father who were waiting for their daughters when the bomb went off. The nurses had put them beside each other for comfort.

Andrew had seen the mother wake up and reach her hand out towards the father, who was still unconscious. It could have easily been him, Andrew thought, as he watched the couple lying side by side. And in a way he wished it was – he would have done anything in the world to swap places with Lisa.

Xander had been quiet for the past few weeks. He was no longer a boy. The night of the bomb had turned him into a man. He caused no fuss and wanted to help his father. He asked all the right questions about Lisa, and accepted it was not the right time to see her.

By the end of the first week in hospital, the ICU team decided to start weaning Lisa off her ventilator, allowing her lungs to take some of the strain to see how she coped.

Louise, a woman in her thirties, and one of the kindest and most gentle nurses on the ward, was given the task. Andrew stood beside Lisa's bed, holding her hand, as Louise began the process of reducing Lisa's dependency, bit by bit, giving Lisa's lungs the chance to take over.

This was another huge moment. There was not a single doctor or nurse in the hospital, not even Professor Lees, who could predict what was going to happen next.

The *woosh woosh* sound of the ventilator became slower as it was gradually dialled down. The minutes ticked by. Andrew hardly dared ask.

He looked up at Louise, who was standing by the ventilator, reading Lisa's life signs on the monitor. A smile began to spread across her face. "She's taking her own breath," Louise said.

It had worked. Lisa's lungs were adapting to being

weaned off the ventilator, and the signs were good that she would be able to breathe on her own.

Now all they had to do was wake her up.

*

Andrew sat in an office with Professor Vivien Lees and Jonathan Duncan discussing Lisa's progress. Sam was there, too.

She had been in the hospital for a week now. The trial with the ventilator had worked. They now had an important choice to make and medically speaking, there was no right or wrong answer so the surgeons wanted Andrew's help.

"We need to think about waking her up to see how she responds," Professor Lees said. "The other option is to keep her in an induced coma and carry on operating."

Andrew knew what Lisa would have wanted. "It's time to wake her up."

The surgeons looked at one another and nodded.

On 30 May, 2017, the nurses began to ease Lisa out of her induced coma. Andrew was getting nervous. For most families, the moment when a loved one comes out of a coma is a cause for celebration.

But this would be the moment when Andrew would have to tell Lisa about Saffie.

And he dreaded it more than anything.

The doctors and nurses on the ward knew what Lisa had been through. They knew how hard she had to fight to pull through those operations. And now she was about to be told that her daughter had died from injuries caused by the same explosion.

They had never known a situation like it. A moment so hopeful and yet so bitterly cruel.

Lorraine sat Andrew down to explain to him the process of coming out of a medically induced coma.

"It's a difficult process," she warned him. "Her body has been through a great deal of trauma. Then she's had the operations. And she has been given some very powerful drugs to help with the pain and put her into the coma. The first few hours are going to be really tough, and you have to prepare yourself, Andrew."

Andrew had never seen anybody come out of a coma before. But Lorraine had. Many times. Intensive care psychosis was something that soldiers experienced in war zones, when their body goes into shock from the trauma of their injuries, combined with being administered a cocktail of drugs.

Lisa was being kept sedated with powerful painkillers; along with noradrenaline, which prevents blood pressure from dropping. She was about to be brought back from the very depths of human consciousness. Lorraine had witnessed patients believing they had been kidnapped by aliens and operated on in spaceships.

One patient thought her family members were in fact imposters. Another patient experienced the feeling of being locked in a box in a field where nobody could hear her screaming.

Andrew thought waking Lisa up might take half an hour

or an hour at most. In fact it took around two days for the paralysing agents in her body to wear off, and for Lisa to start waking. A finger would twitch. Or her eyes might flutter. An arm might move, or a leg.

As Lisa began to wake, she became frightened for her safety. She started fighting the nurses. "LEAVE ME ALONE. GET AWAY FROM ME!" she screamed.

Andrew had never seen Lisa act that way in his entire life. Lisa was quite shy in front of people she didn't know. She was calm and collected and reserved, unless she was around her close friends after a couple of glasses of wine, then she could be the life of the party.

But he had never known anything like this.

Lisa was aware that she had been sleeping. It seemed to her that she had woken in a bright square room with locked doors and she was trapped inside this room with strangers. She was convinced she had died and was in limbo. This room was the space between heaven and hell.

She had to get out of limbo. She had to get through one of the doors, but these strangers were trying to stop her.

"GET OFF ME!"

She picked up whatever objects she could find and threw them at the nurses. Andrew did his best to calm her.

"Lisa. Please, it's Andrew ..."

He asked Lorraine to get Professor Lees. Andrew needed some reassurance. He was brought to a telephone at the nurses' station next to Lisa's bed on the unit.

"Professor Lees. It's Andrew. Lisa is going mad."

"What is she doing at this very moment?" Professor Lees asked calmly.

Andrew looked at Lisa. "Right now? She's trying to sit up and grabbing all her tubes, trying to pull them out. She's punching and kicking anybody who's going near her."

"Fantastic. That's great news."

"Excuse me?" *How could this be good news?*

Professor Lees explained how Lisa fighting and punching and kicking was a good sign. For a start it meant she wasn't paralysed. Professor Lees had always been concerned with how Lisa might have fallen at the point of the bomb blast. There had always been a possibility Lisa had damaged her nerves in a way which they did not understand. Carrying out an MRI scan had not been possible while Lisa was attached to a ventilator.

"Give her time," Professor Lees said. "I'll come and check on her as soon as I can."

Andrew and the nurses did their best to keep Lisa calm while the drugs left her system. By eight in the evening, Lisa had opened her eyes and was able to speak and understand what Andrew was saying.

The moment had come.

Nurses began to move away from the bed to give them some space and time on their own. Some of them were visibly upset. They knew what was about to come. They knew what Lisa was about to hear.

Andrew was sat on the bed. He reached for her hand and for the first time she let him hold it.

"They've brought you out of a coma," Andrew said. "You were hurt. You're in a hospital."

Lisa wasn't interested. She didn't care. "Where's Saffie? Why aren't you mentioning Saffie?" It was the first sentence she had said since coming to her senses.

Andrew looked at her. He couldn't speak. He couldn't say the words. But she knew.

"She's gone. Isn't she?" she cried. "Why did you wake me up? I want to die. Please, let me go."

Andrew hugged her as she cried.

Lisa had fought for eight days to stay alive. She had survived a series of life-threatening injuries which had required some of the country's most experienced surgeons to take advice from British Army trauma medics. She had fought her way out of a coma, her last memory being surrounded by doctors and nurses who were cutting her clothes off for surgery.

She had been through all of that: only to wake up into a world in which her youngest child was no longer alive.

That night was the hardest night of their lives. Many married couples would have been left broken by the experience. Indeed, many who experience the pain of losing a child in traumatic circumstances will separate, unable to cope with the pressure of staying together.

But Andrew and Lisa were no ordinary married couple. They were soulmates, brought together by a random twist of fate.

And where there is love, there is always hope.

Chapter 10
A One in a Million

Andrew and Lisa have told the story of how they first met many times. Often they tell it together, both of them cracking jokes about their first encounter, enjoying the look of disbelief on the face of the person listening.

"You're *joking*? I can't believe it!" was the most typical response, followed by, "What are the chances?"

So, how did a property developer from Liverpool who lived in the northwest of England manage to meet a funeral parlour administrator from Nottingham who had never left the midlands?

Lisa was born in Nottingham in 1968, the youngest of three siblings. She had a brother, Stephen, who was ten years older, and a sister, Karen, who was eight years older. She would often get bossed around by both of them. Lisa would joke that – because of the size of the age gap – her arrival had been an accident. She secretly believed it was true.

Her mother, Brenda Bosworth, worked as a carer in a mental health hospital. She was funny, outgoing, and loved to talk and be around people. Her father, Jerzy Komarek, was from a farm in southwest Poland, and worked for the French resistance in the Second World War. He rarely spoke about the war, and it upset him to remember his friends who had died. After the war, he was granted British citizenship, taking the name George Komarek, George being a translation of Jerzy.

George first met Brenda in a pub on Clumber Street, Nottingham. Brenda was supposed to be meeting a friend who never turned up. George was 33 at the time, with dark blond hair and twinkly blue eyes. Brenda was 20, slim and petite, red hair in a bob, green eyes and small features. Their age difference didn't bother them much. They started courting, and a year later, Brenda was pregnant with Stephen.

George worked in the Sunblest bakery in Nottingham. He would come home carrying freshly baked bread in a basket, its sweet smell spreading into every corner of their end-of-terrace house just outside Nottingham city centre.

He was an alpha male, strict, but capable of great kindness, too, and had a daft sense of humour. The family would crack up whenever he wrote the shopping list. SOP instead of SOAP, BRAD rather than BREAD. He would walk around the house singing Shaddap You Face, by Joe Dolce. *What's-a matter you? Hey! Gotta no respect?*

But the war had left its scars, which came out in terrible tempers. Brenda was forced to leave the family home several times, going to her mother's house with Lisa, only for them to return because they had nowhere else to go. "You've made your bed, Brenda, now you have to lie in it," was her mother's advice.

School was an escape for Lisa to a place where she could

make friends and get up to mischief. Like her mother, she was a sociable sort, who mixed easily, and loved to have a laugh.

She had plenty of friends at Elliot Durham Secondary in Mapperley. One of them, Janine, had been a close friend since primary school. Lisa found Janine's antics hilarious. They would swap classmates' jackets on the backs of chairs, causing confusion when the bell rang; drop out of cross-country and go for a smoke in a secret spot, re-joining the pack for the return leg. Janine brought the fun into every situation.

Lisa did well in her exams and passed GCSEs in English, Maths, Biology, RE and Art. She left school at 16 and worked in the office of Age Concern, and after that Scope, the disabled equality charity, where she met a young Shane Meadows, who would go on to become a film director famous for This is England.

By now it was the late eighties and Lisa was enjoying Nottingham's rock club scene. She styled her hair into a big frizzy perm and danced to music by the Human League and Tears for Fears with Janine and her friends Nicola and Paula.

Her first husband was somebody she knew from school. She bumped into him on a night out in Nottingham, they had a quick romance and got married. Lisa was 20. Her first daughter, Ashlee, was born two years later in 1991. They bought a house in Nottingham, and Lisa got a job working in the office of a funeral parlour.

But her relationship with Ashlee's father never flourished into what she hoped it might. They became more like friends, and at the start of 2002, after twelve years of marriage, she decided to separate and later divorce.

Lisa had no intention of plunging head-first into a new relationship. She wanted to enjoy her freedom, spend time with her close circle of friends, and find out what she really wanted out of life.

Then one evening in March 2002, everything changed.

Lisa arranged for her friends, Janine and Dean, to come to the house for a glass of wine and a gossip. They were winding Lisa up about going on a date. She was single, and there was a man – a friend of a friend – who was interested in asking Lisa out for a drink.

Lisa wasn't sure, and instead of agreeing to the date, had deleted the man's number from her phone. Three glasses of wine later, Janine and Dean were on her case.

"Go on, Lisa, just text him!" Janine said.

"It's only a date!" Dean said.

Maybe they were right? What harm could it do? After all, it was only a date!

But there was a slight problem: Lisa had deleted the man's number from her phone a few days ago.

She typed out the mobile telephone number from memory into her phone, writing him a message.

Fancy getting together for a few drinks this weekend?

She hit send. Seconds later, she received a response.

I think you've got the wrong number.

Crap! Lisa messaged back.

I'm really sorry.

Instead of texting her would-be suitor, she had messaged a complete stranger.

Lisa thought nothing of it. Then her mobile phone rang.

A first impression of Lisa would be of a shy and sensible type, happy to listen to the thoughts of others before offering her own opinion. And that is true, of course. But there are many sides to Lisa's personality, and one of them is quite mischievous.

This will show them, Lisa thought.

Janine and Dean stared, mouths wide open, as Lisa picked up her mobile phone and answered the call.

"Hello, Lisa speaking ...?"

*

Andrew Roussos was born in Wigan Infirmary in the late seventies to two hard working parents, who had found success running fish and chip shop businesses in the northwest of England.

His mother, Eleni Roussos, and father, Diomedes Roussos, were both Greek Cypriots, who had moved to the UK in search of a better life. They arrived in London in the mid-sixties, taking the names Helen and Tony, both unable to speak a word of English.

Tony bought a fish and chip van and drove around

factory sites in London, serving the workers at lunchtime. They had their first son, Christopher, in 1966, and by 1970 had ditched the van to run a fish and chip shop in Wigan. The hours were long, and the work was dirty and hard, but there was serious money to be made.

Shortly after Andrew was born in 1973, the family moved from Wigan to Hunts Cross in Liverpool. Tony had come across an opportunity to run a fish and chip shop business around the corner from the Ford car factory. The car workers would fill their shop at lunchtimes, and the profits came rolling in.

Andrew grew up around the shop, watching his parents working themselves to the bone. Tony and Helen worked Monday to Saturday, and Sunday was their one day off, by which time they were too exhausted to pay much attention to their sons.

Helen would complain. Her back hurt. Her legs hurt. Tony was pushing her too hard. The money may have been good, but to Helen, her life had become about frying fish and peeling potatoes in a city far away from sunny Cyprus, which was still home.

By the time Andrew was nine, Tony and Helen moved back to Cyprus. Helen had finally got her way, and Tony had agreed to give up the business. They had made enough money to build some houses for the family in Limassol, a city on the southern coast of Cyprus, known for its medieval castle and sandy beaches.

Those days in Cyprus were the most carefree of Andrew's

life. He was suddenly free of the shop. He could play with friends, swim in the sea, run free in the clean air.

It didn't last long. When he was 13, his parents divorced, and Tony moved back to England to start another fish and chip shop in Liverpool. Andrew followed his father back to England. He went to a local comprehensive school and hated it. He played truant and spent weekdays in the city centre rather than the classroom, getting up to no good with the other rebels.

He left school with no GCSEs and a teacher's report which said he had wasted everybody's time, including his own. But Andrew was far from lazy. He learnt the fish and chip shop trade from his father. He was a good talker and got on well with the customers. He was 18 when his father went back to Cyprus and he took over the shop with his brother Chris.

They eventually sold the business and went into the property trade, buying up houses for £30,000 each, using a team of plumbers, electricians and decorators to renovate them. They started buying larger houses in Formby, a wealthier part of Merseyside, working on higher value homes.

Andrew had a first marriage which didn't last long. By 2002 he was divorced and single, concentrating on the business, with little time for exploring a new relationship.

One fateful evening in March that year, Andrew was in his brother's house with his sister-in-law, Pat. They were watching a film on TV, while discussing plans for their property business. The conversation turned to Andrew's love life. "You need to get on with your life," Pat told him.

"I know, I know," Andrew said wearily. Then he received a text.

Fancy a few drinks this weekend?

Andrew looked at Chris and Pat on the sofa. "You guys are so obvious."

"What?" Chris blinked.

"You must think I was born yesterday! Fancy a few drinks this weekend?" Andrew said, reading out the text. "Is this a wind up?"

It wouldn't be the first time his brother had pranked him. Chris once gave Andrew's details to the local radio station, Radio City. Liverpool's legendary local DJ, Tony Snell, had called him up pretending to be a driver who had accidentally reversed into his Mercedes. "I'll get my mate to fix it," Snell told him live on air.

"What do you mean you'll get your mate to fix it! It's a fifty grand Merc!"

"You sound angry."

"Just wait there!"

"I've got no insurance."

"Oh, here we go!" Andrew fumed.

Andrew's hilarious reaction saw the prank voted the scam of the year by Radio City, now called Hits Radio Liverpool.

Andrew could have easily ignored or deleted the message. But instead, he called the number, curious to see what this person had to say for themselves, expecting one of Chris's friends to answer and start panting and grunting down the line.

Andrew called the number. One hundred and ten miles away in Nottingham, Lisa picked up.

Chapter 11
The Scouser and the Chick

"You've got me all excited now," Andrew said. "Who are you?"

"Oh my God," Lisa exclaimed, "I've got a Scouser on the phone!"

Lisa's only experience of hearing a Liverpudlian accent was watching the TV soap Brookside. Lisa could hardly understand him.

Janine and Dean were in hysterics. "Eh, eh, calm down, calm down!" they laughed.

Andrew and Lisa spoke for a few minutes, messing around, Andrew getting stick about his accent. The call ended with Andrew satisfied his brother was telling the truth. It had been a completely random text message sent by a woman in the midlands who sounded roughly his own age. How bizarre!

He sent Lisa a follow up text message.

Great chatting. Hope you had a good time with your friends!

The next morning, Andrew decided to chance his arm with another text.

How did your night go?

That was how it started for Andrew and Lisa. They began telephoning one another, every day, speaking for hours at a time. Both of them had been involved in marriages which had not worked. They were both going through a period of self-reflection in their lives.

What did the future look like? How would they stop making the same mistakes again? Would they ever find the right person?

They had found a non-judgemental and neutral observer in the other person. Sometimes they would talk to each other for so long they would fall asleep with their mobiles on their pillows. Andrew's phone bill one month was £1,000.

Lisa had always been a romantic at heart, being brought up on Disney films, which often had a handsome prince at the end of a long and bumpy road. Well, she had been down that bumpy road before. She had no idea where her conversations with Andrew might lead. But she knew she wanted to meet him.

One evening, Lisa was with Janine when Andrew called. "Why don't you come up now to Liverpool?" Andrew said. "Go on ... I dare you."

"Don't dare me because I will," Lisa shot back.

Janine looked at Lisa. "I can take care of Ash."

"Right, then," Lisa said, "I'm on my way."

"You what?!" Andrew said, suddenly panicking.

"I said fine. I'm on my way."

Lisa had never driven on a motorway before, but curiosity had got the better of her.

This was an era before smartphones or dating apps. They

hadn't swapped a photograph of each other and had no clue what the other person looked like. She was half-expecting him to have black curly hair, a gold medallion and a shell-suit tracksuit.

Would she be attracted to Andrew? Would he be attracted to her? Would they get on with each other in person?

These were the thoughts running through her head when she got into her Peugeot 206 that night and drove up the motorway to meet Andrew in Liverpool. Life was about trying new things and meeting new people, she told herself. *What's the point of living otherwise?*

She had to try.

Meanwhile, Andrew was pacing around his apartment in Crosby, trying to remain calm. He called Chris and Pat.

"You don't even know who she is!" they said. "What if she's a nutcase? Have you never seen Fatal Attraction?"

He booked a room at the Village Hotel, just off the junction of the M57 and M62, and gave her directions so she could find it.

By now Lisa was in full wind-up mode. "Just so you know how to spot me, I've got red hair and boils on my forehead."

Andrew dressed in his best shirt, put on some aftershave, and drove to the car park of the hotel to wait.

He waited and waited. Lisa was nowhere to be seen. He checked the time. She should be here by now. He called her.

"I'm lost," she said.

She had overshot the M62 and was driving towards Toxteth, a rougher part of Liverpool.

He told her to pull over and wait until he arrived. He drove to the road where she was parked. He saw her car. A green Peugeot 206. It was dark, but he could make out a slim woman with blonde hair behind the wheel. He pulled up his car behind Lisa's and got out, his heart beating so hard he thought it might burst.

He took a few steps forward, only to watch in amazement as Lisa drove off down the road.

What the ...?

Lisa had panicked. She had been waiting for so long on her own in the dark that she had worked herself up into a frenzy. *You don't know anything about him! You could end up buried under his patio!*

Andrew called her on the phone. "What are you doing?"

"I don't know," she said, flustered. "I got scared."

"You're heading towards a rough part of town. Just ... follow me in the car to the hotel, ok? Then we'll go inside for a cup of tea. Just a cup of tea and a chat."

Andrew has a knack for reassuring people. He instinctively knows the right thing to say at the right moment. Hearing his voice made Lisa feel better.

She followed him to the hotel car park. He parked up his car and got out. She drove around the car park in circles until she felt safe enough to stop.

Andrew walked up to her. "I feel dizzy watching you drive around in circles like that. Are you ok?"

She nodded. "I think so."

"Let's get you inside for a cuppa, eh?"

They walked into the hotel and had a cup of tea in the bar. They had a long chat, and went to the room, where they carried on talking for hours, face to face at last. Lisa was nervous, and so was Andrew. They had been talking for so many months on the phone they felt like they knew one another.

They lay on the bed, back to back. Andrew turned off the light, and said goodnight. Lisa heard only his voice and felt comforted by it. *Yes*, she thought. *That's Andrew. I'm safe with him.*

They started seeing each other most weekends after that. Lisa would drive up to Liverpool, finishing her job at the funeral parlour on a Friday night or Saturday morning. Ashlee would spend time with her father at the weekends, and stay with Lisa weekdays.

Andrew was 28 and Lisa was 33. Their relationship developed quickly, and by the start of 2003, Lisa agreed to move into Andrew's apartment in Crosby, along with Ashlee.

It was a big decision. Lisa was leaving her life in Nottingham, the only place she had ever lived. It was where her mother and her friends lived, as well as Ashlee's father and Ashlee's friends. The northwest of England may as well have been another country. Lisa has always been a deep thinker, and every big decision she has made in life came with worry and anxiety about whether she has done the right thing.

Was she jumping into another relationship too soon after her divorce? Would Ashlee like her new school? What if Ashlee wanted to leave her and go back to Nottingham?

In those first few weeks after moving, she would drive down to Crosby Beach, sit on the sand, and watch the waves rolling into the shoreline. On a clear day you can see the hills of North Wales from that beach. The sea had always made Lisa feel calmer. There was something about the water which soothed her worries.

Her first marriage had not worked out, but this time it felt different. She seemed to click with Andrew. He was handsome and easy-going with a good sense of humour and he didn't take life too seriously. He liked having a laugh but was sensible, too, and a hard worker.

They both knew what it was like to take a wrong turn in life. But meeting Andrew made her believe that everything happens for a reason. It felt like fate.

A year after moving in together, Andrew and Lisa got married in a small civil ceremony on Liverpool marina, with just a few close family and friends in attendance.

This was their second chance. They had each finally found their soulmate.

Chapter 12
Living the Dream

Andrew had never been a fan of England's weather. The grey clouds and drizzle seemed to last for most of the year. It made him long for the carefree days he spent as a child in Cyprus, swimming in the turquoise seas, his shoulders the colour of honey in the baking sun. "What's the weather like there?" he would ask his family back in Cyprus, knowing the answer, but wanting to hear it anyway.

Lisa, too, has always enjoyed a warmer climate. She first visited Kefalonia with her friend Dawn, and fell in love with the Greek island, made famous by the book *Captain Corelli's Mandolin*. She could picture herself living in a cliffside villa, swimming in the sea, drinking wine in the tavernas.

Ashlee had settled into her new school and made plenty of friends. She had developed a love of heavy rock and thrash metal, and was going through a teenage goth phase. She would be dropped off at her father's house in Nottingham at the start of the weekend in normal clothes, but by the time Andrew and Lisa picked her up on the Sunday, she would be transformed into full goth: black tops, black dresses, black eyeliner.

Andrew and Lisa were not certain if they should have children together, but gradually came around to the idea. It felt like the natural way to continue their love story.

Xander was born in September 2005 at Ormskirk District General Hospital. Lisa was out of the hospital the same day she arrived and could not have hoped for a better birthing experience. Her baby boy – she had always wanted a boy – turned out to be a great sleeper, with a surprisingly easy-going temperament for a new-born baby.

Their biggest worry about Xander was that he appeared to stop breathing in his sleep. Andrew and Lisa became paranoid, and would stand over his cot, watching him. They bought a cot-bed alarm which monitored his breathing in the night and they even went to the GP about it. "We're watching him at night, and it looks like he's holding his breath?"

The GP, who was completely unconcerned, said: "You know the solution to this problem, don't you?"

"No?" they said.

"Stop watching him at night!"

Two years later, Lisa fell pregnant again, and this time it was a girl. Lisa would have liked to call her Sofia, but Ashlee was against it. She had a friend with the same name she had fallen out with. The name was no longer an option for her new half-sister.

Sofia was adapted to Saffie, which became Saffie-Rose. In the years to come she would only be called Saffie-Rose when she was in trouble. *Saffie-Rose! Stop jumping off the sofa!*

From the very start Lisa knew she was going to be the sort of child who was always on the move. She was constantly wriggling about in Lisa's tummy, prodding her with an elbow or a foot.

Lisa was due on 15 July, 2008, but the doctors became worried about Saffie's positioning. On 4 July, Lisa was booked for a caesarean section at Ormskirk Hospital. She was kept under local anaesthetic, as the medical staff used clamps and tools to pull Saffie out, marking her head in the process, which upset Lisa, even though the marks would soon heal. Afterwards, the nurses lay Saffie on Lisa's chest. She was six pounds and nine ounces and she was perfect in every way. One of the nurses took Saffie away to give Lisa a break. Lisa wouldn't have it. She asked for Saffie back. She never wanted to be apart from her.

She wanted to be with Saffie, always.

*

Once Saffie was born, Andrew and Lisa started talking more about moving to Kefalonia. They wanted to raise their children in a warm climate where the world and its troubles couldn't touch them. They had watched the hit musical film Mamma Mia! on TV – which was about life for a family on a Greek Island. They wanted that life.

Why couldn't it be them?

They came up with a plan. Andrew could sell his properties in his property business and they could use the money to buy a block of holiday apartments in Kefalonia, which could be rented out to holiday makers. But this was

2008. The world was going through a financial crisis and the UK's property market had crashed. They could wait until the market had recovered or they could sell up and make their dream a reality.

They decided to sell.

Instead of making about half a million pounds clear profit, they were left with £80,000. It wasn't a huge amount of money, but they were determined to make it work.

In October 2008, Andrew, Lisa, Ashlee, Xander and Saffie got a taxi to Manchester Airport and waved goodbye to the UK. They arrived in Kefalonia and enjoyed a short holiday before planning for their future on the island. They had found an apartment block in Sami in Kefalonia which they could buy. Sami was a port town where tourists would stay in apartments for a week or two over summer. Andrew and Lisa would run the apartment block on behalf of the tour operators.

They sorted out a loan with a Greek bank but when the purchase was about to go through, the bank cancelled the loan agreement. Many European countries at the time had large debts, but Greece was one of the worst countries affected because it had borrowed more money than it was able to repay in revenue through taxes. The banks were now in trouble and cancelling on loans. The deal for the apartment block collapsed.

No matter. They had savings, and were determined something would turn up. Maybe the chance to run a sandwich shop in some town square, or maybe a café?

Andrew was from a long line of family members who ran their own businesses and shops. The family would joke that the reason they set up their own businesses was because they couldn't stand working for somebody else, and nobody else could stand them.

After a couple of weeks on the island, Ashlee decided to return to the UK. Kefalonia was too sleepy for a 17-year-old. She wanted to go back home to Nottingham. Lisa was devastated. But she understood Ashlee's reasons, and Ashlee promised to visit regularly.

They moved to a village called Moussata, between Skala and Argostoli, the island's capital. They set up a clothes shop, spotting a gap in the market for affordable clothing on the island.

Some of those days were perfect. In the mornings and afternoons they would run the shop, then in the evenings socialise in the bars and restaurants, Andrew riding the coastal roads on his Harley-Davidson motorbike with Lisa on the back.

Saffie loved shop life. She loved being fussed over by the customers. As she got older, she would toddle about the aisles, and clamber up onto Andrew's Harley, which was parked in the men's section, centre-stage for the display. Saffie loved to dance and perform for her parents. At one Christmas party in a bar full of ex-pats Saffie got up off Lisa's knee, toddled to the dance floor on her own, and started dancing. Soon enough, everyone had joined her.

They loved their lives in Kefalonia. But the recession hit

hard, and the shop was not making enough money. They had £15,000 left in savings, and knew they had to leave. Andrew's father, Tony, said they could come to live with him while they got back on their feet. They said goodbye to their friends and left the island for Cyprus.

The family spent eighteen unhappy months in Cyprus before moving back to the UK. Andrew's mother paid for their flights, and they returned to Manchester Airport on a cold snowy day in the winter of 2010. Xander and Saffie had never seen snow before.

It was all one big adventure to the children. Andrew and Lisa had never allowed their money worries to trouble them. But privately, they were scared. They had arrived in the UK with just a few hundred pounds left in savings.

They had nothing left but each other.

Chapter 13
Make or Break

The family moved into a rental property in Southport. It was a bare house with empty rooms. No sofas, no beds, no glasses or cups, or cutlery in the drawers. Nothing. Still, Xander and Saffie ran about like crazed banshees, excited at the idea of living in a new house. For Christmas day, they went to Poundland for toys, and had Christmas dinner from Lidl.

They were flat broke. Andrew needed to get a job, quickly. His uncle, Mike, offered him a job serving behind the counter of his fish and chip shop in Liverpool for £6 an hour. Now was not the time for being fussy or proud. Andrew took the job, and turned up for work on a freezing cold day without a jacket. The next day, Mike bought him one from Primark.

Mike and his wife, Nicoletta, did everything they could to help Andrew and Lisa, and when Mike heard about an empty café in Bootle, one of Merseyside's more deprived areas, he introduced Andrew to the owner.

The café owner needed somebody to run it for him. Andrew and Lisa jumped at the chance, thinking that Andrew could cook the food, while Lisa could take the orders and serve the customers.

This sounded like a simple system, but while Andrew was

used to working in shops, Lisa was more used to working in an office. Serving the customers used to terrify her, especially when she could hardly understand what anybody from Bootle was saying. One time a customer asked for sausage on toast, which is known as "sausage on", and which Lisa completely misheard.

"I'll 'av a sausage on, please, love," the customer said.

Lisa nodded and smiled, then turned to Andrew, who was working the grill.

"Andrew," she whispered. "I think that customer is asking for ... erm ... Szechuan sauce ...?"

In the summer of 2012, Andrew heard about another business opportunity. A fish and chip shop was up for sale on the high street in Leyland, Lancashire. He knew nothing about Leyland other than it was famous for Leyland Motors, a company which made buses. He was warned about the state of the shop before he arrived because the business had been run into the ground, so badly that it had a one-star hygiene rating from the council.

Lisa couldn't believe the filth. They found maggots in the fridge; mayonnaise tubs growing mould spores; tiles thick with black mould; drains full of discarded chicken legs. The asking price was £12,000, and they agreed £10,000. The shop came with an apartment upstairs where the family could live.

Their mission was to turn a dilapidated slum into one of the best fish and chip shops in Lancashire. They had help from Derek, a fish and chip shop fitter, who did everything from electrics to ranges. If you want to set up a fish and chip shop in the northwest of England and need the kit, Derek is your man.

He installed a three-fryer range, bought second-hand from Blackpool; a professional potato rumbler, which is a large potato peeling machine; and a chipper, which creates the chip shapes by passing them through a knife block. Derek paid for the equipment himself up front, allowing Andrew and Lisa to pay him back later.

Andrew refused to remain in poverty. He didn't want that, for Lisa or for his children. He *had* to make this work.

Lisa, who had turned down the chance of being a trainee pharmacist to run the shop with Andrew, painted the outside an off-white, greyish colour. Upstairs they knocked down walls of the apartment, ripped up carpets, painted walls, and scrubbed every inch with bleach.

They called it The Plaice, and it opened to paying customers in July 2012. Once again, the basic plan was that Andrew would cook, while Lisa served. But if Lisa struggled with the Liverpudlian accent, then she was lost in Lancashire.

"Pea juice."

"I'm sorry, what?"

"A corn of chips."

"Excuse me?"

"Scraps."

"Pardon?"

"Baby's yed, please."

"Errr ..."

One day the doors opened, and in walked Chloe, a young girl from the town, who wanted to know if they had any shifts going. Chloe was sixteen, five feet seven inches tall, wore her hair in a bobble, and was an all-round chip shop legend.

Chloe taught Lisa about Lancashire slang, portion sizes, how much salt and vinegar to put on, how to wrap the chips properly, how to serve lots of people and remember their orders. Lisa grew in confidence, and was soon able to run the shop front, while Andrew cooked.

Saffie, who was four by now, thought Chloe was the coolest thing to walk the planet. Chloe knew *everything*! Saffie would get back from pre-school and climb up Chloe's leg like a koala bear and cling to her back while she was serving customers. Saffie was like an extra appendage.

As the business took off, Andrew and Lisa hired more staff to help them out. First there was Chrissy, a local woman in her thirties, whose adding up was occasionally a concern to Andrew and Lisa. Four portions of fish and chips, costing £3.50 each, would come to £8.50. "Er, Chrissy, I'm not sure that's right ..." Lisa would say, delicately, asking her to try again.

But she was loyal, which was a big positive, as far as Andrew and Lisa was concerned, and she worked hard.

Jan was another worker who was hired after Chrissy, and another loyal and valued hard worker. She bred rottweilers in her spare time and could be extremely abrupt with the customers, to the point where it became comical. "What do *you* want? Come on, hurry up, I haven't got all day …? Chips and gravy, is it?"

Andrew caught her sticking a pudding in a microwave – instead of steaming it properly in a pan – which meant it was served frozen solid on the inside with hot gravy poured on top. After that she was banished to the kitchen, where she would wash the pots and tidy up.

Saffie would wash up next to her, bossing her about. "You've missed a bit!"

"Thanks, boss," Jan would say.

Running the shop was hard work. Lisa was on her feet every day, peeling potatoes, washing up, serving customers, scrubbing the kitchen, and cleaning the pots. Then there was the matter of raising two young children.

They had swapped their dream life on a Greek island for a six-day hard working week in a fish and chip shop in Lancashire. Maybe it wasn't the dream they had always hoped for. But they were happy. That was enough for them.

Chapter 14
Saffie's Surprise

The Roussos family spent Christmas Eve 2016 at home in Leyland. Xander and Saffie watched Polar Express, a film about a mysterious magical train which picks up a young boy on a journey to the North Pole. Ashlee was there, too. Craig had dropped Ashlee off for her traditional Christmas Eve stay over. She enjoyed watching Xander and Saffie open their presents.

By now, Xander was eleven, and Saffie was eight, and their bickering could be awful. A few months earlier they had been screaming at each other so much in the yard at the back of the shop that a member of the public had complained to the police that "somebody was doing something terrible to two children". Two uniformed police officers turned up. Xander and Saffie emerged looking sheepish, asking their parents if they were going to prison.

"Yes. You're going to jail," Andrew said with a straight face.

On that Christmas Eve, Andrew and Lisa spent ages chopping vegetables in the kitchen. Andrew's Christmas dinners could have fed an army regiment; in front of them were heaps of carrots, sprouts, broccoli, potatoes, cauliflower, and parsnips.

As the evening wore on, it became obvious that Saffie

wasn't keen on going to bed. What was the point? She wouldn't be able to sleep, anyway?

"You've got to get to sleep before the ten o'clock horses come," Lisa warned.

The saying was from Lisa's mother and Lisa had no idea what it meant. But it seemed to have the same effect on Saffie as it did on her when she was eight years old.

Saffie nodded. Oh yes, the ten o'clock horses! I forgot about those!

They left Santa a mince pie and a glass of milk, and a carrot for Rudolph, placing them on the stairs down to the shop.

Once the children were in bed, their parents began to arrange their presents under the tree. Saffie had trainers, a toy dog, make-up and nail kits, Ariana Grande perfume, colouring books and pens, a blue Nintendo DS console and a Pokémon game.

Xander had a Nintendo DS and a full-sized drum kit, set up in the kitchen downstairs.

The next day the children leapt out of bed and ran for their presents, wrapping paper flying everywhere. Saffie would always count each present to make sure she had an equal amount with her brother – it didn't matter how big or small each present was, Andrew and Lisa had to make sure they had an equal number.

Downstairs in the shop kitchen was another present for Xander. A full-size drum kit.

"No way!"

He pulled off the wrapping paper, picked up the drumsticks, and started bashing.

Saffie stood watching her brother, smiling.

"What's that, Saffie?" Lisa said, pointing at a white envelope on the sofa, where they had a small living room space in the kitchen set up for the shop staff.

Saffie picked up the envelope, looking confused. At first sight, a white envelope, no matter what it contains, can be a disappointing sight for an eight-year-old whose brother had just received a drum kit.

She opened it up and took out three tickets. She held them in her hand, not understanding, looking up to her mother for an explanation.

"The tickets are to see Ariana Grande," Lisa said. "She's coming to Manchester."

"Ariana Grande … is coming to *Manchester*?" Saffie said, her little nose wrinkled in confusion.

Lisa had to explain.

Ariana Grande, Saffie's favourite singer, was coming to Manchester as part of her Dangerous Woman tour. And Saffie was holding three tickets to her concert in her hand.

The penny dropped. Saffie's face transformed before their eyes, from disappointment, to screaming with excitement.

"OH. MY. GOD!"

Andrew and Lisa and Ashlee laughed at her reaction. Saffie was so loud and dramatic, the very opposite of her brother.

She ran up the stairs. "I'm calling Lily."

Saffie and Lily were inseparable. Every evening after school they would meet to play in their parents' shops, or on the pavement outside, where they would watch Ariana Grande videos on their mobile phones, taking turns to endlessly bounce around on a pogo stick.

The tickets costed £138 each. Lisa bought three. One for Saffie, one for Ashlee, and one for herself. Over at Lily's house, her dad, Mike, checked for tickets to see if Lily could join them, but the tickets had already sold out.

The date of the concert was 22 May, 2017, at the Manchester Arena. Saffie told everyone about it. She told her classmates, her teachers, the customers in the shop, everyone she possibly could.

Her obsession with Ariana Grande had grown from watching her in Victorious, a children's sitcom about a performing arts high school in Hollywood. Ariana played one of the characters, Cat Valentine. Saffie loved the spin-off show, Sam & Cat, which also starred Ariana. She would watch those shows over and over again on TV.

This had evolved into listening to Ariana's pop songs. She would cut pictures of her out of magazines and put them up on the walls of her bedroom and on her dressing table.

At the same time, Saffie was doing well at school. Her teacher suggested she might like to run for the school council, something she took extremely seriously. She devoted herself to her election campaign and bought a roll of stickers, writing on each sticker: VOTE SAFFIE.

She made a canvassing board which read: WHO'S DONALD TRUMP? VOTE FOR SAFFIE!

Her classmates were convinced. Saffie duly won the election and she got to wear a pupil councillor badge. She had also decided to start learning the trombone, which came as a surprise to her parents. One afternoon, Andrew and Lisa waited for her in the car park outside school and watched in amazement as Saffie walked out with a gigantic black case.

Andrew and Lisa stared at her as Saffie walked towards them. "Saffie, what on earth is that?" said Lisa.

"A trombone. I'm going to learn it."

Of all the instruments, she had picked the largest and noisiest one available.

PARP PARP PARP ...

Andrew quickly banned her from playing it during shop opening hours.

Saffie had become a confident and outspoken girl, and although she could cause mischief and take the mickey, especially out of her father, who she called Mr Bean, and brother, who she loved to film on her mobile phone just to annoy him, she also cared about people deeply, and had an unusual amount of empathy for an eight-year-old.

Once, Saffie caught a cold in school, then a few days later Lisa became ill with a vomiting bug and had to stay in bed to get better. Andrew found Saffie in her bedroom, sobbing into her pillow.

"What's the matter?" Andrew asked.

"I've made mummy sick!"

It took her parents hours to convince her that it wasn't her fault that Lisa was ill. And only then did Saffie stop crying.

That's the sort of child she was. She liked rough play but was affectionate. She would give you a hug which would almost knock you off your feet. She had a habit of writing little notes to her mother and father and hiding them around the shop and apartment for them to find. The notes would read: "I love you mummy" and "best daddy ever", decorated with love-hearts and kisses.

One time she cut out a love-heart shape from grease-proof paper and gave it to her father, who was working behind the counter in the shop. It made his day.

*

The pop concert was on a Monday. Lisa had picked that day, rather than the Tuesday concert, because Monday was a quieter day for the shop. She would feel less guilty about leaving Andrew on his own.

She had so nearly bought the tickets for Tuesday. In the years to come, she would think about that decision, and every other decision which led her family into the City Room in that exact moment on that exact evening in May.

What if?

Lisa knew she could spend her life asking such questions. But it was impossible not to think it.

What if they had left before the encore?
What if they had stayed a few minutes longer?
What if they had stopped off for the toilet on the way out of the arena?

On the morning of Monday, 22 May, Saffie went to school, as usual. As soon as she was home she ran upstairs to start trying on outfits, pulling open various drawers, clothes flying everywhere. Lily arrived to help get Saffie ready.

They picked out a white Dangerous Woman tour T-shirt which had a picture of Ariana Grande in black and white; a blue denim skirt with black leggings; Converse trainers; and a leather jacket.

Ashlee arrived at the shop with Craig, her boyfriend, a nightclub manager from Southport. Craig would drop them off outside the arena, then Andrew would pick them up.

Saffie came downstairs into the shop. She had her hair in a high ponytail, the way Ariana wore it. It was the first time she had worn it like that. Normally her hair was loose and down over her shoulders, or in a ponytail when she was at school. Everybody said how gorgeous she looked.

"Wait one minute!" Saffie declared.

She ran back upstairs. She came down a few minutes later wearing her black suede ankle boots, rather than her Converse trainers. She thought they made her look taller and more grown up.

It was about 5pm. Lisa, Ashlee and Craig were waiting for her outside the shop. Saffie bounced past the shop counter, where Andrew was busy serving a customer. Saffie was just about to walk out the door.

"Are you not saying goodbye?"

Saffie ran back and gave Andrew a big hug, one that almost knocked the breath out of his lungs. "Goodbye."

"Have a great time. Send lots of pictures." Saffie was running out of the door. "I love you," Andrew shouted.

"Love you," she said quickly, and disappeared.

Andrew turned back to serving the customer.

In the years to come he would often think of that goodbye.

Chapter 15
Ariana

June, 2017

Lisa Roussos's first week in hospital had seen her endure the unimaginable, both physically and mentally. She had been through life-saving operations, only to be brought out of a coma and told her daughter had died. She knew she had to carry on for Ashlee and Xander, but deep down Lisa felt she should have died with Saffie.

That feeling did not take away her fight to recover. She knew she had to keep fighting, for the sake of her children.

But it would linger, a kind of guilt she couldn't quite shake. It meant she rarely made a fuss about her treatment and recovery, and asked very few questions about herself, which included waiting four days after coming out of the coma to ask Andrew if her right hand had been amputated. It was bandaged up, and because she was unable to feel it, she assumed it was no longer there.

"Your hand is still there, babe," Andrew told her.

Andrew and Lisa had become close to many of the ICU nurses. They were the sort of couple who made friends wherever they went in life, and they remain friends with some of the nurses to this day. They swap stories with Lorraine about Lisa's out of character behaviour on the ward, when she was still high on painkillers and morphine. Like the time Andrew was out shopping with Des the police officer and he got a call from Sue, one of the nurses.

"Lisa's grabbed my apron and won't let go of me until I give her some water."

Andrew turned up to find Lisa clinging onto Sue like a monkey. He didn't know whether to laugh or hit the panic button.

"I need some water!" Lisa said.

"You're nil by mouth!" Andrew said.

"I'm not letting go until I get some water!"

Lorraine arranged for some orange and lemonade ice lollies to be brought to the ward. Strictly speaking, patients shouldn't have lollies if they were nil by mouth. But it would do no real harm.

The very next day, Andrew got a phone call again. "Andrew. It's Sue. She's grabbed me again!"

By mid-June, Andrew decided it was time for Xander and Ashlee to see their mother. Xander had been waiting patiently every day for this moment.

Lisa made herself look as presentable and sat up in bed as Ashlee and Xander entered the ward. Ashlee was in a wheelchair, still recovering from her operations. She wheeled herself over to her mother's bed and reached out for her. They hugged and Lisa stroked her hair. Ashlee cried. They didn't say Saffie's name. They didn't have to.

Xander sat on the bed. "Are you alright, mum?" he said.

"I'll be fine. What have you been doing? Have you been looking after your dad?"

They chatted away about nothing, as families do.

Lisa lay in bed, listening to her children, knowing that she could never leave them. Saffie's loss was a burden she would have to bear for the rest of her life, but she was determined to bear it, because she was a mother, and always would be.

*

For the past few weeks, Andrew had been living in a bubble created by the hospital and his police liaison officer, Des, but it had not escaped him how much criticism Ariana Grande had received for going back to the US so soon after the attack.

"It's not fair," Andrew told Des one day. "She's only a young girl. She probably wanted to be with her family, same as the rest of us."

Des shrugged. "True enough."

Andrew had an idea. "I'd like to meet her."

"Seriously?"

"Seriously. I'd like to meet her. I think it's important."

Des was an experienced police liaison officer, with many years of dedicated service. But arranging a meeting between a family and an international pop star was way out of his comfort zone.

A few days later, Des arrived at the hospital with a grin on his face. "She wants to meet. Tomorrow."

Ariana Grande was arriving at Manchester Airport at 2pm on a private jet. She would be driven to Sedgley Park Training Centre in Prestwich, where Greater Manchester Police (GMP) trains its police officers and newest recruits.

Des drove Andrew and Xander to the centre. The main building was a grand old Victorian house. The dining room had a portrait of Queen Elizabeth II on the wall.

Ariana was late. It was 5.30pm and Lisa would be wondering where Andrew was.

"I need to get back for Lisa," Andrew said.

"Just give me five minutes," Des pleaded. "We're going to blue-light her from the airport."

Ariana Grande arrived twenty minutes later. Andrew, Xander and Des had to leave the dining room while her bodyguards carried out a sweep. When they went back inside the dining room, Ariana was sitting on one of the sofas, and Scooter Braun, her manager, was standing in the middle of the room.

Braun was known for discovering Justin Bieber, the Canadian pop singer, along with some of the biggest names in music. Andrew shook his hand. 'I'm sorry for your loss," Scooter said.

Ariana stood up and walked over to Andrew. She was small and dainty, only five feet tall while Andrew was six feet two inches. She put her arms around his waist and hugged him.

"I'm sorry," she said, over and over, tears running down her cheeks.

Andrew thought nothing of her celebrity. She was a lost and confused young woman, trying to cope with what happened. And she didn't deserve any stick for the arena bombing.

Andrew took Ariana by the hand and sat down next to her on the sofa, his fatherly instincts taking over. "This isn't your fault," Andrew told her. "Saffie loved you. And she had the time of her life watching you on stage. I'm grateful she got to see that before what happened."

"Thank you," Ariana said, wiping the tears.

"You can't go through life blaming yourself. This wasn't your fault. And nobody blames you for it," Andrew said.

Ariana nodded. Andrew told her about Saffie watching her in Sam & Cat, the volume turned up to max on the TV.

Ariana grinned. "And who's this?" she said, looking at Xander, standing close by.

"This is Xander. Saffie's brother."

"Hey, Xander." She stood up and hugged him. "Do you like school? What are you into?"

"Pokémon Go."

"No way! I *love* Pokémon Go!"

Xander and Ariana chatted, while Scooter Braun pulled Andrew aside. "This will mean the world to her," he said quietly.

Andrew nodded. After a few minutes they said goodbye and got back in the car. They needed to get back for Lisa.

Des turned to Andrew. "Absolutely brilliant. That couldn't have gone any better."

Andrew felt better for doing it. He hoped his words might mean something to Ariana. But above all, he wanted her to know the arena attack was not her fault.

Chapter 16
In the Killer's Footsteps

As more information was starting to emerge about the bomber, Andrew was receiving regular updates from Des about the police investigation. He and Lisa cared very little about the man with the rucksack. Lisa simply refused to give him any headspace. What was the point, they reasoned, in filling yourself full of hatred for somebody who had been brainwashed like that?

The criminal investigation into the bomb had started approximately two minutes after its detonation, when the police received its first 999 call from a member of the public. At 11.27pm Simon Barraclough, a detective chief superintendent, received a telephone call at home from Temporary Assistant Chief Constable Russ Jackson.

"There's been a bombing at the arena," Jackson said. "It may be a suicide bombing. We need you to come in."

Barraclough had joined Greater Manchester Police in 1988. Most of his service had been spent investigating homicides and suspicious deaths. In 2003 he became a senior investigating officer leading major incident teams in murder investigations around the Manchester area. From 2005 to 2007 he worked in Northern Ireland carrying out counter-terrorism operations. He was in charge of an investigation into poisonings at Stepping Hill Hospital by a nurse and was also in charge of the investigation into the murders of two female police constables, Nicola Hughes and Fiona Bone, by a one-eyed gangster.

By March 2014, he was appointed head of investigations for the Northwest Counter-Terrorism Unit. He was sent to the FBI in the United States to train on a post-blast investigation course. He was a highly experienced detective, and it was to him that GMP looked to catch those responsible for the arena bomb.

Barraclough headed to a secret base for counter-terrorism investigations shortly after midnight on 23 May. The Prime Minister herself wanted to know whether or not there was a network responsible for an attack on British soil, and if so, was it planning more attacks on our towns and cities?

An estimated 1,000 police officers, police staff and National Crime Agency officers would work on the investigation. And it was Barraclough's job to make it run effectively.

At an early stage, he set six main objectives for his team. They would identify any continuing threat to public safety; find any further offenders who were a threat or might have helped the attack by any means; identify the bomber; secure the bomb scene and gather the evidence; find relevant eyewitnesses; and identify the victims and deploy family liaison officers to their families, such as Des.

He needed to get answers about this bomber – who he was, and who he was connected to. He asked Robert

Gallagher, an expert in forensic and digital investigation, to get down to the arena and take charge of the scene.

"I want that scene forensically sealed," Barraclough told Gallagher in the situation room.

Gallagher entered the smoking charred remains of the room in the early hours of Tuesday morning. The ceiling looked unsafe. It was made from large plate glass panels which looked like they could drop on people's heads at any moment. It was a risk to work in the room, but Barraclough needed answers. The Prime Minister herself needed to know if the country was safe.

And the first clues would be here in this very room.

Gallagher set up a common access path – a sort of platform where the forensics team would walk up and down to cause the least amount of disturbance to the crime scene. At precisely 1.58am, while walking along the platform, examining the rubble, something caught Gallagher's eye. A small rectangular object in the debris, sitting near one of the box office windows.

Gallagher stepped towards it, picked it up and dusted it off. It was a Halifax bank card.

And the bank card read: *Salman R Abedi.*

Gallagher called Barraclough from the scene. "I think we've found something, boss ..."

Abedi had been arrested for shoplifting in 2012. Police had his photograph, fingerprints and DNA on file. They matched those to what remained of his body.

Gallagher discovered that triacetone triperoxide explosives had been used in the improvised explosive device found in Abedi's rucksack, an explosive known as "Mother of Satan" which is easy to make if you know how, using certain amounts of hydrogen peroxide, acetone, and sulphuric acid. The precise recipe is of course restricted knowledge.

This information would help Barraclough. He needed to find out how Abedi had sourced those particular chemicals as it would tell him more about any possible terror network.

Gallagher's people worked quickly. At 10am the ceiling came down, and he evacuated his personnel. He had done his job. Barraclough had what he needed to set his detectives loose on the case.

Hours later, Ian Hopkins, the Chief Constable for Greater Manchester Police, stood outside force headquarters, and addressed the waiting media.

"I can confirm that the man suspected of carrying out last night's atrocity is 22-year-old Salman Abedi ..."

The hunt was on.

*

By June, Lisa was ready to move from the intensive care unit (ICU) to the burns unit in the ward next door. This was a big step forward as it meant the doctors and nurses believed that Lisa could now cope without round the clock care. But for Lisa, the move was devastating. Nurses Lorraine, Sue, Rosie, and Jo, had become her friends. She trusted them. They had a routine. Lisa knew how the ward worked. She didn't want to go to a strange ward with nurses she didn't know. Trust was hard earned with Lisa. It took her time.

Leaving ICU felt like she was losing the people who had saved her life. She cried and cried and cried.

One evening, Sue and Rosie sat her down to explain the reasons for moving her.

Lisa wasn't having any of it. "I'm just going to discharge myself, then," she said.

"If you discharge yourself where are you going to go?" said Sue.

Lisa looked up. "Your house!"

"*My* house?" Sue said.

Sue looked at Rosie then back at Lisa. The three of them burst out laughing.

A few days before she left the ward, the nurses rigged up a TV next to her bed and they watched the One Love Manchester benefit concert. Ariana Grande and Scooter Braun had organised the 4 June event to raise money for the We Love Manchester Emergency Fund, which had been set up by the city council to help the victims and their families.

More than 55,000 people attended Old Trafford Cricket Ground to watch Justin Bieber, Coldplay, Miley Cyrus, Liam Gallagher, Katy Perry, Take That and Robbie Williams.

Des told Andrew and Lisa he could arrange a private box for them if they wanted to go. But Lisa was having an operation, and Andrew and Xander didn't want to go without her. They watched it on the ward instead with the doctors and nurses who had helped them so much in the past week.

Ariana Grande sang One Last Time.

Andrew watched her singing on TV and remembered a moment back in the apartment in Leyland. Saffie was on the sofa, listening to songs on her mobile phone, singing the words.

One Last Time ... I need to be ... the one ... who takes you home ...

"What's that song called, Saffie?"

"One Last Time."

"Play it again," Andrew said. Saffie hit repeat. Andrew thought it was quite catchy. "Do you like this one?"

"Yeah, course. But it's not my favourite." Saffie looked up at Andrew. "But it can be our favourite song, dad."

Opposite Lisa was the young mother who had also been blown up by the arena bomb when picking up her children. Her partner, who had been in the bed beside her, had been moved to another part of the hospital. She was lying there, alone, covered in bandages, watching the concert on TV.

Andrew went over and hugged her. He didn't say anything. He just held her hand for a moment, then went back to Lisa's bed.

Chapter 17
Letters

Learning to walk again was a painful process for Lisa. Every day two hospital physiotherapists would come to do her exercises, and every day Lisa was left exhausted. They attached metal braces to her legs, which worked like a splint to keep her legs aligned. The braces made it hard for Lisa to balance. It was like having scaffolding attached to her.

The physios took it slowly. At first Lisa would have to shuffle to the side of the bed, swing her legs over, and stand up on her own. Then she would sit down. Then stand up again. Then sit down again.

This was repeated, over and over, until they were confident Lisa could stand up and balance on her own.

Next, Lisa had to take a couple of steps away from the bed, walking down the ward, with a physio either side in case she lost her balance. Each day Lisa would walk a few more steps, building her confidence and her stamina. After that she was being given an apparatus which looked like a Zimmer-frame on wheels.

Andrew couldn't help but take the piss. "You're like an old lady going down the shops," he laughed.

"Oh, bugger off, you," Lisa said. And she would go off down the corridor with her Zimmer about twenty metres, turning around and coming back again, her body pouring with sweat.

The physios pushed her hard. "One more time?" She would never refuse. She wanted to restore her mobility as best she could. She didn't want to be wheelchair bound.

She walked down the corridor, again and again with that apparatus, until the sweat dripped down her brow, then she would climb into bed, exhausted. The pain was so great she would need an injection of morphine before every session. Pain was something she has had to learn to live with. It has improved over time, but has never gone away.

Xander would walk with his mother up and down the corridor, going one step at a time, as she pushed her Zimmer-frame.

By July she was walking on her own, without help from the apparatus, physios, or family members. She was on a programme designed to improve the strength and flexibility of her arms and legs, doing stretches, and visiting the hospital's rehabilitation room, which was like a gymnasium for people recovering from accidents and injuries.

She used the parallel bars to help her walking, and a block which had three small steps up to a landing and three steps down again. Lisa would pump her body with morphine before this exercise. Stairs were painful for her legs.

Physically, she was starting to recover. In terms of the mental trauma she had suffered, she had not begun to process Saffie's death, and tried to push it away. She could not contemplate the idea of Saffie having suffered or been in any sort of pain. She had not asked for any details of what happened to her after the explosion, and neither had Andrew. It wasn't something they could cope with at that time.

In their minds, she had died instantly, without fear or pain. She was there – there was a flash – and then she was gone.

They had received some very strange letters from members of the public since the arena bomb. One of them had been a little threatening, and a mini police inquiry had been launched into its origins. The police never got to the bottom of who sent the strange letter with Arabic writing to their shop in Leyland. But it highlighted the need for security.

Lisa was sent another letter which revealed to her a number of graphic details about what happened to Saffie after the explosion. Reading the letter caused her such intense pain she was left short of breath.

Her brother, Stephen, came to her bedside as she read it and saw how distraught she was. "Lisa? What is it?"

Silently, she handed him the letter. Stephen read it. His face turned pink with anger. Andrew and Des arrived. Stephen passed them the letter.

Andrew read it. He took the letter and walked away. When he came back, he said he had torn it up and thrown it into a bin.

Des was livid. He had been working hard behind the scenes to make sure life was as easy as possible for the

Roussos family. This letter had slipped past all his efforts, through no fault of his own.

Andrew had not been in his shop since the visit to the apartment with Xander the day after the bombing. There were countless jobs to do in order to halt a fish and chip shop's operations, as Des was quick to find out. Stock in the fridge needed to be cleared out: pies, peas, beans, batter, curry sauces, salads, and butter. The fish delivery had to be cancelled, and so did the weekly sacks of potatoes from the potato merchant.

Then there were the administrative hiccups. Like when Andrew called up BUPA, the health insurer. They had full insurance before the arena bomb. Andrew knew Lisa was going to need additional care at home and he wanted to know what BUPA could offer.

He called up the helpline number and explained the situation and what had happened to them. "I'm sorry, Mr Roussos," the young man explained, "but your policy doesn't cover terrorist attacks."

Andrew told Des about what had happened. Des gave him a look. "We'll see about that."

Andrew had no idea what Des did, but the next day he received a phone call from a senior executive at BUPA, who apologised profusely for the misunderstanding. Lisa would be covered by BUPA and the resources of the private healthcare specialists would be at the family's disposal, she said.

Des also put Xander in touch with Once Upon A Smile, a Manchester-based charity which helps children going through bereavement. The charity organised days out for Xander: a trip to an indoor ski slope, a Star Wars exhibition, and visits to McDonald's. It meant the world to the family.

They also got a visit from Ian Hopkins, the Chief Constable of Greater Manchester Police, who came to see them at the hospital. He put his arms around Andrew. "I'm so, so sorry," he said, looking genuinely upset.

Hopkins visited Lisa's bedside. He asked about her recovery and again apologised.

He said his officers, being led by his best detective, Simon Barraclough, would find out what had happened. "We will bring the right people to justice. That is my personal promise to you."

In July, Andrew, Xander and Tony were moved into a furnished bungalow on the hospital grounds. The hospital had bungalows for the families of people who were long-term patients, and the accommodation was far more comfortable than being in a room inside the main building. It had a large bedroom with two single beds and a pull-out bed. There was a bathroom with a shower, a living room and kitchen. There was even a washing machine and dryer. Ashlee and Craig were moved into a bungalow next door, so the family could be together as they recovered.

Andrew was grateful for what the hospital had done for

his family, but he knew it could not last forever. At some point, they were going to have to go out into the world on their own again and he was worried how Lisa would cope with that given how dependent she had become on the protective bubble and support provided by the hospital.

Even having a bath would take two hours. Andrew or the nurses would undress Lisa's bandages, wash her, then wrap her up again in fresh bandages. Dawn, one of Lisa's closest friends, would often give her a bed-bath, turning up every morning at 6am, such was her dedication to her friend.

Lisa would hear Dawn's flipflops slapping along the corridor, and she would sit up, feeling reassured that Dawn had arrived. She cared for Lisa every single day, and Lisa would always feel grateful for what she did.

But what would happen when Andrew and Lisa and Xander were left on their own? Where would they go and how would they manage? Andrew knew they couldn't return to the shop and pick up life again in Leyland. That was gone now. That was their old life.

They needed a fresh start.

*

Des walked into the bungalow one day holding a letter. "Not another bill?" Andrew said.

"No. Read this," Des said, handing him the envelope.

On the front was a red stamp reading: Buckingham Palace.

"Bloody hell!" Andrew said.

It had been a tough few months. 4 July had marked what would have been Saffie's ninth birthday. Instead of celebrating by holding a party for Saffie, Andrew found himself doing an interview with BBC Radio 4's Today programme, which had just under eight million listeners at the time.

"We've lost everything," he told the programme. "We have, we've lost everything, because life will just never be the same." He said the family were speaking for the first time so as not to let Saffie's birthday go by unmarked. "Saffie loved the limelight and I just wanted to celebrate Saffie's birthday through doing this ... her dream was to be famous."

Lisa was finding her recovery hard and was taking a lot of painkillers to cope. She had a bottle of morphine which she sipped on constantly, like it was a can of Coca-Cola.

How had their lives come to this, Andrew thought?

Not that long ago he was working in a fish and chip shop in Leyland and life was straightforward. Now he was living in a hospital, doing interviews on Radio 4's Today programme, and getting letters from the Royal Family.

He wanted his old life back. More than anything. But that wasn't going to happen.

He opened the letter. At the top were the words "Highgrove House", the private residence of Prince Charles, who is now King Charles, since his mother died.

He read the letter.

Andrew was amazed. It was a genuine, heartfelt letter from Charles. Completely different to the almost robotic letters which had come from Downing Street.

Charles and his wife Camilla wanted them to know "how deeply we feel for you and your poor family", and shared a personal memory about their own experience with loss. Charles wrote about his own family member, Lord Mountbatten, his great uncle, who had been blown up in an IRA terrorist attack.

"Therefore, I can at least understand something of what you are going through and my heart goes out to you more than you can possibly realise," wrote the future King. "Above all, we wanted to assure you that you and your family are so much in our special thoughts and prayers at such a very difficult and utterly devastating time."

Andrew showed the letter to Lisa. They were both moved that Charles had set aside the time to write it and astonished and touched by how personal it was. Charles's family, too, had been victims of terrorism, once. He had recognised a shared bond.

Chapter 18
The Longest Walk

Andrew spent his time going back and forth between the bungalow and the burns unit. Lisa would remain there until the end of July and was then moved into the bungalow. Before then, Lorraine, the ICU nurse, wanted to do something fun for Lisa which would get her out of the hospital.

Lorraine told Lisa she was going to a Coldplay concert. Lisa said how much she loved Coldplay, and so Lorraine promised to bring her back a programme.

When Lorraine was at the concert, she wrote a note and gave it to a security guard backstage. She said she was an ICU nurse looking after Lisa Roussos, the mother of Saffie-Rose Roussos. The next day, Lorraine received an email from Coldplay, offering Lisa and her friends VIP boxes to their Cardiff concert in July.

The hospital and Professor Lees were against the idea. Professor Lees didn't feel like Lisa was ready and was worried about infection and her mental health going to a concert venue. But she was eventually convinced because Lorraine and Jo, the ICU nurses, were going with her, and it was going to be a private box with special security.

Lorraine even messaged her favourite comedian and writer, Stephen Fry, who provided the family with chauffeur driven cars and a hotel in Cardiff. Lisa met Chris Martin backstage before the show. He said the arena attack had affected him deeply, and he was very sorry for what happened to Saffie.

Later that night, he sang Everglow, telling the crowd, "I would just like to say we've got Saffie's family here tonight and they were involved in the Manchester bombing. I would like to dedicate this song (Everglow) to Saffie-Rose, the youngest victim."

The entire audience switched on the lights on their mobile phones and waved them from side to side in tribute. Coldplay fans will say the song makes them think of family members they have loved and lost.

But when I'm cold, cold
In water rolled, salt
I know you're always with me
and the way you will show
And you're with me wherever I go
And you give me this feelin', this everglow ...

"I need to leave," Lisa said, after the song ended. "I need to go back to the hospital."

Andrew and Lorraine had felt the visit had been important. Lisa's recovery would depend on her keeping up her spirits and her morale, as much as anything physical. The concert was about giving her something to look forward to. Lisa, they had noticed, was becoming nocturnal, something which is common in patients who have been in an induced coma. She was scared of falling asleep in case she returned to that limbo state: that locked room with the closed doors.

She would sleep in the day, when she knew family and nurses were around to keep her safe, then stay awake at night, when it was quiet, forcing her eyes to stay open.

Her body, however, was growing stronger, even though she had been given a customised wheelchair to get around the hospital because the muscles on her legs had wasted.

Lisa also struggled to look at her reflection in the mirror. She had been lucky that her face had not been scarred by the blast. Her worst affected area was the back of her legs and she was shocked when she first saw them. She had been avoiding looking at them, until one day, she asked Andrew to get a mirror while her bandages were being changed.

"How can you look at them? How can you touch them?" she asked Andrew after seeing her legs for the first time.

"Don't be daft, they're fine," Andrew said.

Lisa just wanted to feel normal again. But for all the physical pain, it was nothing, absolutely nothing compared with the pain of losing Saffie.

A date loomed large on the calendar, one which Lisa had been trying not to think about. It would take every ounce of her strength to get through.

*

The funeral was set for Wednesday, 26 July, 2017. Saffie's service was to take place at Manchester Cathedral, right in the city centre, close to the arena, and Andrew and Lisa had a meeting with Reverend Canon Marcia Wall, who prepared them.

Saffie's godmother, Nikki, and her husband, Antonis, wanted to sing. They were professional singers who performed in restaurants and bars in Cyprus. Saffie adored them, and would ask them to record their performances and send the videos. They wanted to sing a Bruno Mars song and Marcia said that was fine. Andrew and Lisa wanted the mourners to bring a single rose for the service and to wear colourful clothes rather than the traditional black.

A big screen was organised for the street outside. Marcia knew it would become a day of mourning for the city and the country – thousands were expected. Andrew and Lisa wanted a big event because they knew it's what Saffie would have wanted.

She had wanted to be famous one day. She enjoyed being the centre of attention. And everything her parents did, they did so with her spirit in mind. Andy Burnham, the Mayor of Greater Manchester, asked if he could attend. So did Ian Hopkins, the Chief Constable, and Downing Street wanted to send representatives of the Prime Minister from London.

That month had already seen many of the funerals of the 22 who had died. Saffie was the last of them to be laid to rest.

Lisa's former boss, Nigel, a funeral director in Nottingham, provided a fleet of Rolls-Royce Phantom cars free of charge, which were driven up on the morning of the funeral. Nigel arranged the cars, as well as a wicker coffin for Saffie, made bespoke, with roses threaded through every part of it. Stephen Fry's chauffeurs offered to ferry people to and from the church, free of charge. Mike, Saffie's best friend's dad, organised a coach to come from Leyland, because of the numbers who wanted to attend. British Airways flew Andrew's family over to the UK.

There was one hitch. Andrew wanted Des to attend the funeral. He had become Andrew's rock. But he had been removed as the family's liaison officer because the hospital trust's bereavement team, who had been involved with Andrew and Lisa's aftercare, were concerned that Andrew and Des had become too close. A manager had become convinced that Andrew might suffer another loss when Des went onto his next job. Andrew fought against the decision but was overruled.

Andrew wanted Des there for the funeral. If he couldn't have Des's support going forward, then the police could at least give him that.

He met with Chief Constable Hopkins at headquarters. Hopkins had said the door was open if he needed anything. Andrew explained the situation, and Hopkins listened. Des would be allowed to attend the funeral, if that's what Andrew and Des wanted, he said.

The sky was overcast that morning when the hearse drove into the grounds of the hospital and parked outside the bungalow. Inside were Lisa's sister, Karen; her brother, Stephen; Andrew's brother, Chris and his wife, Pat; Dawn and Sam, Lisa's closest friends; Ashlee and Craig; and Andrew's father, Tony. Andrew's mother, Helen, was unable to attend due to serious illness.

Andrew went outside. He walked to the back of the hearse, where the wicker coffin sat.

"Open it, please," he told Nigel.

Nigel opened the hatch at the back. Andrew reached out his hand and touched the wicker coffin. It was his first time being close to Saffie since she said goodbye to him. He closed his eyes and breathed. He needed to summon the strength to get through the day.

Around him, the doctors, nurses and patients were walking out of the different buildings of the hospital and standing quietly, lining the pavements and the roads. They stood in unison – not saying anything – paying their respects. Andrew recognised many of the doctors, surgeons and nurses who had looked after the family.

He closed the hatch.

"Let's go," he said to Nigel.

The hearse and Rolls-Royce cars were escorted by police motorbikes, front and back, blue lights flashing. Andrew held Lisa's hand. They knew what would be waiting for them at the cathedral. The car parked up in front and Andrew got out.

There were thousands of people. Each one of them standing holding a pink rose and dressed brightly.

In a corner was the world's media, TV cameras pointing towards the cars, the reporters on standby. Andrew had asked for the families' faces not to be filmed, but for the filming to be taken from behind, as they walked in and out of the church. Sky News was the only media organisation allowed inside the church.

Lisa sat inside the car. She was a private person but she knew there would be no private moments for her today. There would be no space to grieve for her daughter. That would have to come later.

Slowly, Saffie's coffin came out of the hearse. Andrew and Stephen carried it at the front, then Tony and his brother, Chris, at the back, and they walked gently into the church.

Back in the car, Lisa's heart was pounding. Every step she had made, walking up and down the hospital corridors, had been for this moment, the one she knew would come, when she walked into the church and down the aisle for Saffie's funeral. She had been determined not to do so in a wheelchair. She would do it standing on her own two legs, no matter how heavily she limped. She would do that for her daughter, and in defiance of the act of evil which had been committed. She would show them that she was stronger. That Saffie was stronger.

Lisa loved her daughter. She loved her, and Saffie had known that she was loved. She got out of the car, stood up straight, and walked into the church.

Chapter 19
A New Life

Andrew wondered about moving to Australia, and mentioned it more than once. He couldn't face moving back into their apartment, and a move around the world would certainly be a fresh start, far away from the northwest of England. Every single part of the shop and flat reminded him of Saffie. The lamppost she would climb and slide down, hanging upside down and pulling faces at him through the window when he was serving customers. The homeless person on the corner she would give a portion of chips. The sink where she would stand on a stool and wash the plates with the staff.

Too many memories.

Andrew and Lisa left the business and it was bought by an old customer. They considered moving to Formby and even put a deposit down on an apartment.

Then at the end of August 2017, Lisa's sister, Karen, invited them to a cottage in Dorset.

They left the hospital and drove to the village, where a chalk stream runs through arable farmland, in countryside which had once inspired Thomas Hardy.

The longer they stayed, the more they started to think about moving there. In the northwest, people recognised them in the street. Here, they were anonymous.

They drove to a nearby beach to watch the waves come into the shoreline. They had been a normal family who ran a business in a small town in Lancashire, quietly going about their lives. Now everything was different, forever.

For a long time after the funeral they didn't talk about Saffie. They couldn't bring themselves to say her name. It was too painful to talk about her. They were surviving, and it was enough.

They rented a house in Poundbury, King Charles's experimental estate in Dorset, which he started building in the 1990s. The estate had a focus on beauty and architecture and while some people love it, others compare it to being like the set of the Truman Show.

Their move to the southwest of England was made possible, in part, due to the We Love Manchester Emergency Fund, which had raised £21.6million. It was being released in stages to the families and dependants of those killed or injured.

Lisa needed Andrew to provide her with full-time care, meaning Andrew could not work. She was in a wheelchair during this period, although as the years went by, she would be able to walk independently, usually with Andrew close at her side, holding her hand.

Lisa hated the loss of independence. She didn't like the vulnerability of being in a wheelchair. What if she was up a hill and the person pushing it let go? Of course Andrew did no such thing. But still. Just going up the street and back again could feel like a trust exercise.

Xander was enrolled into a school. He kept what had happened to his family and his sister a close secret. His teachers knew, but he didn't want to be treated differently by his classmates. The secret remained, until one of his friends visited his house, and saw photographs of Saffie on the wall.

"You never said you've got a sister?" his friend asked, confused. "Where is she?"

After that, word got around school. It was difficult to escape the reality of their loss.

Saffie was never hidden by Andrew and Lisa. They would always have a bedroom for her containing her wardrobe, chest of drawers and dressing table, and arranged as she used to have it. There were Ariana Grande pictures, and photographs of Saffie with her friends on the dresser. Inside the wardrobe her clothes remained on hangers, in a neat colourful row. Keeping her part of their family helped Andrew and Lisa cope. They didn't want her to be forgotten.

The period they lived in Poundbury was a tough one. The shock was slowly subsiding, and what was left behind was grief: dark and terrible and looming. Lisa's mood could be triggered by anything. The glimpse of a small brunette girl with her mother in the town centre, helping with shopping bags. Ariana Grande's music playing in a café. An anniversary of a significant moment.

Lisa was having dark thoughts, which she admitted to Andrew, and there were times when she did not want to carry on. One day, Andrew came downstairs to find that

Lisa was not in the living room. He searched the house from top to bottom, shouting her name, getting anxious. She had gone out. But she never left the house without him. Her balance had never recovered. He was worried about her falling on the pavement and breaking something.

Andrew opened the front door and looked up and down the street. "Lisa?" he called.

He got into his car and drove around the streets. It was morning and the area was quiet.

There was a dual carriageway close to Poundbury where the vehicles and lorries drove past at high speeds and Andrew drove to that spot, just in case, praying she had not done anything stupid.

He had already lost Saffie. He could not lose Lisa, too. That would be the end of him.

He searched along the streets until he found her, sitting alone on a bench by a field. He parked the car and walked to her. He sat down next to her, without saying a word.

"I need to tell you something," Lisa said. "Please, forgive me, but I can't go on any longer. I've decided to be with Saffie."

It was the first time in months they had said her name. Andrew understood. He was probably the only other person in the world who could.

"I've had the same thoughts myself," Andrew said. "But we've got Xander and Ashlee. They depend on us."

Lisa wasn't particularly religious, but she did believe vaguely that there was *something*. Perhaps a way in which people lived on after they died. And just maybe that's where Saffie was, waiting on her own. Lisa told Andrew that she didn't want Saffie to be alone.

But she also realised something else in that moment. That although she didn't want to be here anymore, she couldn't cause Andrew and Xander and Ashlee any further pain.

It was her duty as a mother to carry on. She had no choice. She had to learn to cope with Saffie's death. It was the only way.

Lisa recognised she needed help, and so went to visit her GP the next day. Her doctor, Steve, whose clinic was in Poundbury, was a warm and upbeat character in his late fifties, who spoke to his patients like they were old friends.

He had been a medic in Cyprus, once, for the Royal Air Force, and was familiar with service personnel who suffered from post-traumatic stress disorder. Steve had been prescribing Lisa with her pain relief medication since they had arrived.

She explained how she had thought about taking her own life.

"I think you're depressed, Lisa," he said.

Lisa shook her head. "I'm not depressed, I can promise you that. I'm just – sad." She told him about leaving the house and Andrew finding her on the bench.

"How do you feel now?" Steve said.

"Different to yesterday."

"How so?"

She thought for a moment, considering the question. "Because I know I can't do it. I know I can't put my family through any more pain."

So she carried on living, one day at a time. Every day.

*

The months after the bomb saw countless newspaper and TV reports about the arena attack. Some of them raised similar questions to the ones that Andrew had swirling around his head.

Why had Lisa and Saffie been left for so long without help? And what did MI5 really know about Abedi before the bomb went off?

For context, the Manchester bombing was not the only terrorist attack to occur in the UK in 2017. Between March and June, there had been four separate attacks in which men used vehicles, knives and explosives to kill or injure members of the public. A total of 36 people had been killed. The Home Secretary commissioned David Anderson QC, who had experience reviewing terrorism legislation for the government, to provide a report on the internal reviews carried out by MI5 and the police after each of the attacks. The government wanted to know if everything was being done to stop these attacks, and what might be learned.

(Author's Note: the QCs mentioned in this book are now KCs, since Queen Elizabeth II died in September, 2022, and King Charles III became king. The author and publisher

have chosen to use QC in the text as that was the correct version at the time of the events described.)

Anderson's report, which looked into MI5's internal review findings, was published in December 2017. The report found that the threat from Islamist terrorism was growing. MI5 officers were seeing the highest tempo of terrorist activity in decades and three of the men in the four attacks had been known to the police and the security services beforehand. Anderson also revealed the scale of the number of people MI5 was having to watch in the UK. At that moment in 2017, MI5, which concentrates on national security, had around 3,000 active subjects of interest, meaning 3,000 people they were watching due to active investigations or an intelligence tip-off about their activity.

Another 20,000 people – equivalent to the population of a small town – had previously been subjects of interest but were no longer in that category, for whatever reason. Perhaps the investigation had concluded, or the tip-off had come to nothing.

At the time of the attack, the arena bomber, Salman Abedi, had been a closed subject of interest, according to Anderson's report. But here was the part which made Andrew and Lisa sit up and take particular notice. MI5 had received some intelligence about Abedi in the months before the attack which, had its true significance been understood, would have caused an investigation to be opened.

Anderson said it could never be known if such an

investigation could have thwarted Abedi's plans to blow up the arena. MI5 claimed it might have given them a slim chance.

But how slim was that chance, in reality?

On two separate occasions in the months prior to the attack, MI5 received intelligence about Abedi. That intelligence has never been revealed for national security reasons.

Anderson's report was enlightening, but it only went so far. Andrew and Lisa's battle for the truth had only just begun.

Chapter 20
Rosebud

The Roussos family have always been determined to keep Saffie's name and memory in the public eye. Saffie had wanted to be the most famous girl in the world, and that meant Andrew and Lisa felt like it was now their job to maintain her memory. One idea Lisa had was to create an original rose flower which could be named after Saffie. She was in Manchester receiving more surgery for her hand when she dropped in to see Marcia Wall at Manchester Cathedral, who had been so supportive.

"Have you thought about having a rose cultivated for Saffie?" Marcia said.

This was the exact same idea Lisa had – which meant it must be a good one. One of the family's nicknames for Saffie was Rosebud, so it felt right. A rose in her name was something which would outlast them all.

Lisa got in touch with the Royal Horticultural Society (RHS) who recommended some rose growers. One of them was Keith Jones who ran a specialist rose company based outside of Chester. He suggested a pink grandiflora, a hardy rose with a quick growth rate. It would be called a "WEKgrasucejuc", or "Saffie-Rose", which would become commercially available for people around the world. The naming rights would cost £10,000.

Lisa set up a JustGiving page in order to fund the costs of the new rose. She hated asking people for money. But she decided to get over her pride and her nerves.

She set up a page one night, writing: "I am the mummy of the beautiful little Saffie-Rose who was tragically taken in the Manchester bombing attack. I have approached the RHS to ask them if they would create a rose in memory of Saffie.

"I spoke to a very lovely man who said he hoped we would get in touch as he too feels it would be a beautiful and fitting tribute to her. The cost of this would be approximately £10,000."

She posted the appeal not knowing if a single person would donate any money or care about her appeal. The first donation arrived minutes after she posted. It was from a man called Barry Greene.

"I'll start this off today," he wrote. "Saffie so deserves a special rose to honour her name x". He donated £30.

Then Darren Green. "A little donation now to keep it going ... but in weeks to come more will be added." £30.

More kept coming. "Hi Lisa, I have made a donation but it would be my pleasure to run our local half marathon in the summer ... I will organise sponsorship forms nearer the time. Thinking of you all," wrote John Loizides.

Charlotte, the mother of Olivia Campbell-Hardy, who died in the arena bomb aged 15, donated £100. "From my angel Olivia to your angel xxxx love to all the family xxxxx."

Lisa checked the Just Giving page every day. She showed Andrew, Ashlee and Xander who could hardly believe it.

People they had never met were offering to do charity fundraisers, raffles, school bakes, and marathons. A school in Burscough, Lancashire, which had five pupils at the concert on the night of the attack, organised a non-uniform day, raising £698.

Lisa broke her target of £10,000. In the end they raised almost £15,000. The extra money was donated to Once Upon a Smile, the charity which had supported Xander.

The appeal gave Lisa a project. It was something positive to focus on in the New Year.

Her hand was still giving her quite a lot of pain and she needed to have specialised therapy. Sessions happened three times a week at her local hospital, where they focused on exercises to improve her grip.

Her now badly damaged right hand had always been the dominant one, so she had to retrain herself to write with her left. Gradually her writing improved. Tying shoelaces or doing up buttons was more of a problem. Andrew had to cut up her food with a knife and fork.

Retraining her left hand to be her dominant hand had some strange side effects. One minute she would be holding the remote, the next she would throw it across the room at the wall. Andrew would stare at Lisa, and Lisa would stare at her left hand. It was like it had a mind of its own.

The hand exercises in the hospital were painful and Lisa would dose up on morphine before going. The physios would force her fingers to bend, trying to improve her grip. Another piece of equipment was a glove which went over her hand with a band attached to each finger which she could tighten individually to stretch the scar tissue. Lisa would have to wear that glove all the time, apart from at bedtime, and she called it her "monster hand".

The family were getting help from the Victim Support charity. A support worker called Krissy was navigating their benefits, food shopping, paperwork and bills. They also hired solicitors to lodge a claim with the Criminal Injuries Compensation Authority (CICA), which was set up in 1996 to provide a compensation scheme to victims of violent crime in England, Scotland and Wales. It was funded by the Ministry of Justice, and the Justice Directorate in Scotland.

Lisa's claim would be based on her loss of earnings. She was 49 and would never work again. Andrew could no longer run a business to support the family as he had to look after Lisa. Their claim was first lodged with the CICA in August 2017 and Lisa was required to go through a number of assessments. She felt as if they were designed to try to catch her out – to see if she might be exaggerating her injuries to get more money.

The CICA commissioned orthopaedic surgeons and expert witnesses to carry out reports on Lisa's condition, looking at her injuries, the treatments she had received, the effects on her lifestyle, and what treatments she would need in the future.

Lisa's head injury had resulted in continuing headaches. She struggled to concentrate at times and suffered from memory loss. She found it hard to remember shortly before and after the attack. Much of what happened to her in hospital remained fuzzy. Shrapnel injuries to her neck and chest and injuries to her legs needed ongoing physiotherapy and rehabilitation. She was taking pain relief medication, including morphine, pregabalin and gabapentin.

One of the assessments found she had "severe restrictions to her mobility" and "remains on long-term pain management". She was registered as disabled and was claiming disability benefits for the first time in her life. She found it extremely difficult to walk up and down any stairs.

The initial CICA offer was in the tens of thousands. It was nowhere near enough to support them through a lifetime of not working and Andrew and Lisa were forced to take the CICA to a tribunal, which eventually sat in December 2023 – six years after the bomb. A judge determined that they should receive a vastly higher sum. The money was eventually paid, following a seven-year legal battle with the CICA, in July 2024.

After the claim was initially filed, in 2017, it was in a sense just another battle the family had to fight. But it was nothing compared with what was to come.

*

In July 2018, Saffie's rose was unveiled to the public at the BBC's garden inside the RHS Flower Show at Tatton Park. The family were brought to a flower bed by the organisers where the flowers were pink and blooming. Lisa touched her nose on one. It had a delicate smell. More like a peony than a rose.

In such ways, the family would keep Saffie's name in the public eye. For the first anniversary of the arena bomb they organised a procession of Harley-Davidson bikes to ride from Preston to Manchester. Andrew used to take Saffie into the Harley shop in Preston, where she would buy badges and stitch them to her leather jacket.

Then in 2019, Lisa took part in the Greater Manchester Run, which was scheduled a few days before the second anniversary of the arena attack. Lisa walked, rather than ran, along 10k route through the city, and was held up by her physio, who was based at the Manchester Institute of Health and Performance, an organisation which had helped Lisa every step of the way with her recovery, allowing her access to their state-of-the-art facilities. She was also supported by 20 family members and friends who were raising money for the charity 22 MCR, which was set up to support victims of terrorism.

The run begins on Portland Street and heads southwest towards Old Trafford, heading back along the same route to finish on Deansgate, a row of shops and bars which cuts through the city.

This was a huge moment for Lisa. After she came out of hospital in 2017, the impact of her injuries meant she never thought she would be able to walk so far. But she did, helped around the way by Professor Lees, who took part, along with the ICU nurses.

At the start of the race Lisa grabbed her best friend, Sam, and drew her close. Sam, who was physically fit, and often ran marathons, had been there for Lisa through the best and worst of times. She was a friend who Lisa trusted and knew she could count on, more like family. Sam had known and loved Saffie, too. She was going through her own grief, but she had never stopped quietly supporting Lisa.

The media had come out in numbers. Lisa had quietly and unwittingly become a symbol of defiance against terrorism, refusing to be beaten by an act of unthinkable evil.

"And here comes Lisa Roussos, walking today in memory of her daughter," said the live race commentator as they neared the finishing line. "What a story of hope and inspiration after what she went through."

The audience cheered as Lisa approached, blowing on horns and whistles, banging on drums.

Despite the physical pain, Lisa had no choice but to finish. Her family and friends joined hands and held them high in the air in solidarity as they prepared to cross the finishing line. As the end came nearer, Lisa was exhausted. It had taken every last bit of her strength to get this far. She was a few metres out, now. Her legs felt like lead, her feet like two concrete blocks.

"And now she's here. Running for the charity 22 MCR ... ladies and gentlemen if you ever need inspiration in life, there it is right now ..." the commentator roared.

The city or the country would never forget what Lisa had been through. Or her courage.

Chapter 21
Secret Justice

In January 2018, the family was making a fresh start in Dorset, trying to look to the future. But they knew there would be an inquest or a public inquiry into the circumstances around the arena bomb and they were not looking forward to it. The legal process was completely out of their comfort zone. They had no idea what to expect. In fact, they were tempted to leave the UK and live in Cyprus until it was all over.

They were still considering doing that when they walked into the lounge of a Holiday Inn in Manchester at the start of 2018 for a meeting with their solicitors, Broudie Jackson Canter. The firm had a strong reputation in the northwest of England for being unafraid to take on the authorities, whether that be the police or central government.

They had already met Elkan Abrahamson and Nicola Brook, two of the firm's most experienced solicitors, who had made them feel comfortable, while at the same time seemed like the sort of people who would push the authorities to get the answers they needed. Abrahamson, who had heavy stubble and spectacles, was the firm's director and specialised in inquests and public inquiries. He was being helped by Brook, who was a veteran of the Hillsborough Inquests, which examined the circumstances around the deaths of 97 people following a catastrophic crowd crush at a football match at Hillsborough Stadium in Sheffield in 1989.

There was a third man in the meeting that day. Andrew and Lisa had never met him before, but his reputation went before him. Pete Weatherby QC was a human rights barrister who practices in public inquiries, inquests, prison and police law. An exceptional lawyer with a brilliant mind, Weatherby was classed a Tier 1 leading silk by the Legal 500, which produces a league table for barristers.

He led a team representing 22 of the bereaved Hillsborough families at the Hillsborough Inquests, and continues to act for their campaign to get the Public Authorities (Accountability) Bill 2017, otherwise known as the Hillsborough Law, enacted. The law would introduce a duty of candour for public servants to address the defensive culture across much of the public sector.

Weatherby also represented 80 of the victims of the Grenfell disaster, and had taken human rights cases relating to the US, Kashmir, Bahrain, UAE, Turkey and Mauritius. He had none of your swaggering barrister's bluster. There was very little ego about the man. He had a slim and average build, with a side parting of light blond hair, and a sharp pair of pale blue eyes.

His voice was not booming, but it was precise and demanded to be heard. Everything about him appeared completely reasonable and trustworthy, which was probably why judges allowed him to explore areas of cross-examination which many other barristers would not get away with. He was a steady ship for families who found themselves in rough waters.

Weatherby stood up, introduced himself, shook hands with Andrew and Lisa.

He recognised in them what he had seen in countless Hillsborough families who had been repeatedly lied to by the police over what happened at the 1989 disaster. He saw they were a family reaching out for answers and some semblance of justice.

Weatherby also realised within minutes of meeting them both that this was a family prepared to go all the way. Andrew and Lisa were not going to stop until they got those answers. Most importantly, they wanted to know if the emergency services had failed their daughter, and if she could have been saved.

"We need to know the truth," Andrew said.

Weatherby nodded. "I understand. And I'm going to do everything in my power to make sure you get it."

The group discussed the difference between an inquest and a public inquiry. Put simply, an inquest was a fact-finding process which determines the cause of death of an individual or individuals. A public inquiry is a major investigation into issues of serious public concern, such as a disaster or a terror attack.

An inquest focuses on the death itself, the immediate causes and circumstances. But a public inquiry could cover a wider range of issues. Public inquiries have legal powers, for example, to compel witnesses to give evidence, which might be important, especially when it came to the bomber's family and associates, and MI5.

A public inquiry is designed to establish the truth and restore confidence by making recommendations to stop similar events from happening again. Weatherby believed it was the right option for the family because it would have the power and scope to uncover more about what happened. There were many powerful organisations which had to be held to account, including SMG, the arena operators; Showsec, the arena security firm; Greater Manchester Police (GMP), one of the largest police forces in the country; British Transport Police (BTP); the ambulance service; the fire and rescue service; and the security service, MI5.

GMP had publicly praised the officers involved in the arena response, even putting forward one of its officers, Chief Inspector Dale Sexton, for the Queen's Police Medal for Bravery, for his efforts in co-ordinating the emergency services response to the attack. He had also been promoted from inspector to chief inspector.

The Kerslake Inquiry, commissioned by Andy Burnham, the Mayor of Greater Manchester, in order to examine the emergency service response, had been highly critical of the fire and rescue service for its failure to play any meaningful role that night.

Those findings were published in March 2018. Kerslake found that the first fire engine did not arrive at the scene until two hours after the explosion. By that time there had not been a single survivor left to save. Their stretchers went unused.

Fire chiefs had been worried about sending in their firefighters into an area where terrorists might be active. Compare this to New York's firefighters during the September 11 terror attack, when hundreds had died running into the twin towers, only for them to collapse. They became national heroes for their efforts. Manchester's firefighters, by the admission of their own fire chiefs, had become a "laughing stock".

GMP was given a softer ride by the Kerslake Inquiry. Dale Sexton, an inspector responsible for co-ordinating the emergency response, had been praised for his "dynamic decision making" in an "extremely stressful, chaotic and dangerous environment".

Privately, however, fire chiefs were furious. Their officers had been unable to contact Sexton because his phone line was too busy. The police's systems had been overwhelmed through lack of preparation and planning, and the communication across the three emergency services that night had been awful.

But the public narrative was already being shaped. The fire service had failed on the night, whereas the police had apparently made the best of an impossible situation. GMP put Sexton forward for a medal, which he received from Prince William in March 2019.

Weatherby believed a public inquiry had the best chance

of getting the answers the families so desperately needed and Andrew was keen for the inquests or the public inquiry to take place as soon as possible. But they were put on hold by the criminal investigation into Hashem Abedi, the younger brother of Salman, who was being held in Libya.

In July 2019, following negotiation by the British government, with the assistance of GMP, he was extradited back to the UK to be charged with the murder of 22 people along with counts of attempted murder relating to those injured in the attack, and conspiracy to cause an explosion likely to endanger life.

It was a huge result for detective Simon Barraclough, whose team had gathered evidence linking Hashem to purchasing the chemicals and preparing the bomb used by his brother. In August 2020, he was jailed for a minimum of 55 years. Being under 21 at the time of the bombing, Hashem was too young for the law to allow a whole-life sentence.

Hashem insisted throughout the trial that he was innocent and on the day of his sentencing he refused to leave his jail cell. But he later confessed in prison to helping his brother make the bomb, though Hashem was no criminal mastermind. He was a dozy and dim-witted young man, nicknamed "Goofy" by his friends, after the cartoon dog, smoked cannabis and had a series of menial cash-in-hand jobs at restaurants and takeaways.

His conviction meant little to the Roussos family. For

them, justice meant holding Britain's authorities to account, not a confused young man from south Manchester.

On the day of his conviction, the family was in Cyprus, visiting family. They had once considered staying in Cyprus until the public inquiry was over. But something had changed in them. They felt stronger, now. They wanted to fight.

Andrew's phone rang when they were on the beach. It was Nicola Brook, their solicitor.

"How long did he get?" Andrew said.

"Fifty-five years minimum."

"Good," he replied. "Time to crack on with the inquiry."

The criminal case was over. Now the inquest or public inquiry could finally happen.

By September 2019, Sir John Saunders, a retired High Court judge, had been appointed to act as chairman of the proceedings, which would start as an inquest, but had the potential to develop into a public inquiry, if Sir John requested one from the government.

One of his first tasks was to deal with an application from the Home Office and GMP to hear some of the evidence in secret. They were asking for public interest immunity (PII) on the grounds of protecting national security. In a two-hour hearing at Manchester Town Hall, both organisations claimed that hearing parts of the evidence about the arena bomb in public could jeopardise national security.

This raised questions for the families. Some of the evidence was going to be embarrassing for the police and MI5. Of course they would want it to be heard in secret, said the families. It would mean they could not be criticised.

"We are dealing here with information which would be of value to those intent on doing the public harm, and would hamper the work of the security services in keeping the public safe," argued Sir James Eadie QC, on behalf of the Home Secretary.

GMP's barrister, Alan Payne QC, backed him up. He said that counter-terrorism police officers had reviewed the material in question and that it "cannot be discussed without jeopardising security."

"National security may not be the concern," said John Cooper QC, a barrister representing some of the families, "but instead, national humiliation."

Sir John Saunders had an important decision to make. He had to balance the expectations of the public in justice being seen to be done, with national security concerns. He also had to consider Article 2 of the European Convention of Human Rights, which is enshrined in UK law. This means the government has to take appropriate measures to safeguard life, taking steps to protect you if your life is at risk.

It meant the scope of the inquiry had to be broad, looking at not only how each person died, but also in what circumstances.

An inquest could only go so far in order to do this. A

public inquiry would have the powers to consider secret material from MI5 and the police – even if it was behind closed doors. Sir John could summon the witnesses he needed, including Britain's top spies. Then he could provide the public hearings with a summary of what he had heard, taking into account national security considerations.

The decision to hear MI5's evidence behind closed doors was a tough compromise for the families. Many of them – including Andrew and Lisa – believed there was a risk of them being able to hide evidence behind closed doors.

Sir John insisted this would not happen. He was a retired high court judge leading an independent inquiry. At least he would be able to see all the evidence and provide a redacted summary for the families and the wider public.

It would give him and the inquiry the chance to probe the conduct of counter-terrorism officers and MI5's intelligence officers. And his conclusions about their missed opportunities to stop the arena bomb would cause more anger and fury for the families than the security service could possibly imagine.

*

In November 2019, Pete Weatherby and Nicola Brook arranged with Andrew and Lisa that they would fly down to see them. By now they had received a large amount of medical disclosure relating to how Saffie had died. Brook had spent weeks piecing together the timeline of Saffie's final moments, and it became clear to her and Weatherby that Saffie had lived for a significant period of time after the explosion. Not only that, but she was conscious, able to speak, and clearly in a great deal of pain.

They knew that because of the length of time she had lived, her survivability would be an issue for the public inquiry and they were certain it would come up during the proceedings. That meant they had to prepare Andrew and Lisa.

Brook and Weatherby decided to fly down to Dorset and deliver the information in person. A few days before his flight, Weatherby was cycling close to his house in Rusholme, Manchester, when a homeless person walked into the cycle lane. He hit the brakes and went straight over his handlebars. "*Ooof ...!*"

Pain throbbed through his hand. He had dislocated his thumb. The day before his flight he had an operation which required a plaster cast to be fitted afterwards. Many airlines require a minimum waiting period after the cast is fitted before flying because of the risk of swelling which can then affect a person's circulation.

Weatherby knew this could be a problem. "I'm flying to Dorset tomorrow," he told his surgeon.

"I don't think that's such a great idea," the surgeon said, bluntly.

"I have to fly. Do what you have to."

The surgeon gave him a specially fitted plaster cast, cutting the underside to give it room to expand. The aircrew accepted the cast was safe for the flight, and Weatherby and

Brook flew down to the southwest of England, arriving on time at Andrew and Lisa's home.

Andrew answered the door and stared at Weatherby's arm. "What the hell happened to you?"

"Don't ask," Weatherby said wearily, walking inside, Brook behind him, lugging both of their suitcases, since Weatherby was unable to carry his own.

Weatherby and Brook sat down with Andrew and Lisa and went through the disclosed material. Brook had been dreading this moment. For good reason. She would later describe that day as the hardest of her professional career, as she and Weatherby described the truth about Saffie's death.

They had discovered that Saffie had woken up around four minutes after the bomb went off. Paul Reid, a merchandise seller, was by her side within minutes. He never left her. He did everything he could to keep her awake, comforted her, gave her some water. He called for help to get first aiders to pay her attention.

Saffie lost a lot of blood from serious leg injuries. She was carried outside the arena by a group of police officers, an off-duty nurse, and Paul Reid. At approximately 11pm – 29 minutes after the bomb's detonation – an ambulance was flagged down, and she was taken to Manchester Children's Hospital. She had asked a paramedic in the ambulance if she was going to die. Attempts to resuscitate her in hospital were not successful. She was then pronounced dead at 11.40pm.

Andrew and Lisa had wanted to believe that Saffie had died instantly. But that was not the reality. The question now, was whether or not she should have been saved.

Chapter 22
For the 22

Sir John Saunders walked into the specially converted room wearing a smart grey suit and a red tie at precisely 9am.

"Would you all please remain standing?" he told everyone, standing at his raised desk. "I shall ask Mr Greaney to read out the names of those who lost their lives. After that we shall observe a minute's silence in their memory."

It was Monday, 7 September, 2020, and the Manchester Arena Inquiry had finally begun. Paul Greaney QC, lead counsel to the inquiry, stood at his desk behind a plastic screen. He had a deep tone of voice, which resonated as he read out the names of the 22 who died.

John Atkinson.
Courtney Boyle.
Kelly Brewster.
Georgina Callander.
Olivia Campbell-Hardy.
Liam Curry.
Wendy Fawell.
Martyn Hett.
Megan Hurley.
Alison Howe.

Nell Jones.
Michelle Kiss.
Angelika Klis.
Marcin Klis.
Sorrell Leczkowski.
Lisa Lees.
Eilidh MacLeod.
Elaine McIver.
Saffie-Rose Roussos.
Chloe Rutherford.
Philip Tron.
Jane Tweddle.

Afterwards the room was silent. Barristers, solicitors, legal secretaries, transcribers, members of the media, assorted family members, and a retired high court judge, stood with their heads bowed in contemplation.

It had not been an easy year. The coronavirus pandemic had struck the UK hard, a silent and stealthy killer which was creeping across the world, passing from person to person, travelling on ships and planes and leaving a trail of death in its wake. The country had experienced unprecedented lockdown measures intended to slow down the spread of the virus which meant restrictions on our freedom.

During that time, Andrew, Lisa and Xander had moved from Poundbury to a rented bungalow also in Dorset. Andrew was worried about Lisa catching the virus and making her condition worse. He had always been known amongst his family for being a little OCD when it came to cleaning and the coronavirus epidemic had sent him into overdrive. Lisa would watch in amusement as he carefully scrubbed each item they bought from the supermarket with an anti-bacterial spray before putting it into the cupboards or the fridge. Tins, cans, toiletries, food in plastic wrappers. He would insist on spraying the soles of Lisa and Xander's shoes with anti-bacterial spray before they went inside the house. Xander would call him a "nutter".

Xander wasn't bothered about the coronavirus. As long as he could connect with his friends online through computer games, he didn't care.

Sam came to visit when the lockdown restrictions had been relaxed and Sam's partner called after she had arrived to say he had Covid. Andrew banished her to the bedroom. He said she had to stay in there until she was clear or go home.

She decided to go home, rather than risk infecting the family. She couldn't face Andrew following her about with a Dettol mist spray. Andrew went into her bedroom and cleaned the entire room with a mask and gloves on, throwing away any cups she had used.

Despite Andrew's best efforts, they all caught the virus, eventually.

Xander got it first. He experienced a light cold and achy muscles. Xander passed it to Andrew, who suffered worst. He was ill for two and a half weeks with flu-like symptoms, losing his taste and smell. He kept his appetite, but everything tasted like cardboard. Lisa was not so badly affected, and managed to recover quickly.

The inquiry went ahead in September despite issues around social distancing. It was held at Manchester Magistrates' Court, which had done its best to accommodate the needs of the chairman, barristers, solicitors, and various witnesses.

Staff had converted two courtrooms into one large room, and some of the desks had protective plastic shields. There were restrictions on the number of people allowed in the courtroom at any one time and families not giving evidence had to watch remotely.

The bible used by witnesses to swear an oath in the witness box had been wrapped in a see-through plastic bag, and many of the court staff were wearing face masks. The media had been placed inside an annexe to the courtroom linked to a live feed, and the proceedings were being streamed on YouTube.

At the top of the room was Sir John Saunders, sitting in a blue swivel chair on the end of a bank of raised wooden desks. He had a computer monitor and two microphones to amplify his voice. Above his head was a sign which read: "Manchester Arena Inquiry" – the word Inquiry written in yellow. To the left of him was the witness box. Then in front were rows of benches containing barristers and solicitors.

Paul Greaney's bench was at the front, folders and

documents heaped on his desk. It was his job to question some of the most important witnesses.

Every night, Andrew would watch the inquiry remotely from his house in Dorset. Lisa found it harder. She didn't want to put herself through every last detail of the worst day of her life. She was happy for Andrew to watch it and update her with the most important information.

Back in inquiry room, the minute's silence was over. Sir John began the hearings with a summary of events. "This inquiry was set up by the Home Secretary to examine the events that led up to the explosion at the Manchester Arena on the 22 May, 2017; the circumstances in which the explosion occurred; and the actions of the emergency services after it had happened," he said.

"The explosion killed 22 people, including children, the youngest of whom was eight years old ... Many, many more suffered psychological injury as a result of being present at the time of the explosion, or from what they witnessed of the aftermath. Many of the survivors will never recover from the effects of what they saw.

"The explosion that brought about these appalling consequences was caused by Salman Abedi detonating a bomb just outside one of the exit doors to the arena in an area known as the City Room. He did that at 10.31pm in the evening as the audience was leaving a concert.

"He chose a place where members of the audience were meeting up with parents and others who had come to collect them. The audience was principally made up of young people. Salman Abedi blew himself up in the explosion. And he intended that as many people as possible would die with him."

Sir John noted that Abedi was already known, at that point, to MI5. "Could and should more have been done to prevent the attack?" Sir John asked the room, his face giving little away. "These are matters we will investigate ..."

The inquiry, he said, would also look at the security arrangements in the arena, as well as the response of the emergency services. "If the response of the emergency services should have been better, would it have made any difference to the chances of survival of any of those who died?" he asked.

The bereaved families and organisations in question each had legal teams to represent them at the inquiry. The families had split into four groups who were being represented by various barristers and solicitor firms.

Two of those groups were represented by Pete Weatherby QC, Anna Morris and Harriet Johnson, who had been instructed by Elkan Abrahamson of Broudie Jackson Canter and Terry Wilcox of Hudgell Solicitors. Andrew and Lisa were part of this group.

Her Majesty's Government was being represented by no fewer than three barristers: Sir James Eadie QC, Cathryn McGahey QC, and Neil Sheldon QC, along with a number of other barristers and lawyers instructed by the Government Legal Department.

The battle for the truth was about to begin.

Chapter 23
Enough is Enough, Sir

Andrew and Lisa set off from their bungalow in Dorset in their black Volvo, feeling nervous about what was to come. It was Monday, 21 September, 2020. Tomorrow they would be giving evidence to the inquiry about their daughter, Saffie.

Each of the families had been asked for a "pen portrait" of their loved one, sketching out their personalities, interests, passions, and what they meant to people. This was important, since it made clear to the wider public the impact of a terror attack.

This was no TV show. This was real life. These were real people, who had lives, and hopes, and dreams of their own, cut short by an act of madness. The voices of those who loved them had a right to be heard, more than any barrister, pre-eminent expert, or judge.

The inquiry had heard that Ismail Abedi, the eldest brother of Salman and Hashem, was refusing to give evidence. He had changed his name and was living in Manchester, in the suburb of Chorlton-cum-Hardy, where neighbours had no idea about his family history.

Ismail claimed he was innocent and knew nothing about the arena bomb being planned. Yet he refused to give evidence on the basis that his answers may tend to incriminate him, the inquiry heard.

To Andrew and Lisa, it was nonsense. If he had nothing to hide, why not come to the inquiry and tell everybody what he knew? Why hide?

The early stages of the inquiry had also heard evidence about British Transport Police (BTP) who were supposed to be patrolling the City Room on the night Abedi let off his bomb. At 7.20pm, two officers visited a kebab shop called Mazaa in Longsight, a round trip of 41 minutes. They took more than two hours for their break.

Abedi first entered the City Room at 8.51pm that night with his enormous backpack containing the bomb. There were no police officers on patrol in the room when there should have been. Instead there were Showsec security guards, hired by the arena: young men with little experience and insufficient training.

Abedi went to the top of a small staircase and hid in a CCTV blind spot at the back of the room for 20 minutes.

At 9.10pm he left the room and went to a Metrolink tram platform. He was hunched over from the 30kg weight of the enormous backpack, walking freely around the empty train station, and sat on a platform, before returning to the City Room at 9.33pm. He went back to his hiding spot in the room – which is roughly the size of a basketball court – and waited there for just under an hour. A member of the public, Christopher Wild, reported him to a Showsec security guard. The guard told a colleague who tried to call his control room on the radio.

By then, it was too late.

It was 10.31pm. Abedi was walking down the staircase, and Lisa, Ashlee and Saffie were walking out of the concert. He mingled with the crowd, then pressed the trigger.

Andrew was horrified by the number of missed chances to stop Abedi, first by the police, who went on a two-hour break to buy and eat their kebabs when they could have been on patrol, then the fact Abedi was allowed to walk freely around a train station with such a huge rucksack, muttering and saying prayers, without being challenged.

Then came the debate between the arena operator, SMG, and their security firm, Showsec, arguing about whose responsibility it was to patrol the tiny bit of space at the top of the staircase in the City Room where Abedi had hid.

SMG bosses said they thought Showsec staff would patrol the area at the top of the steps – where Abedi was sitting. But Showsec believed their patrol duties ended at the bottom of the flight of steps. Showsec said it was not their understanding, nor their practice, for staff to patrol that area, looking for suspicious characters.

This was despite security check lists for Showsec presented at the inquiry reading: "ENTIRE City Room area ..."

It was turning into a blame game which was making Andrew angry.

How could anybody learn anything? How could this be prevented from happening again if each organisation was going to come to the inquiry and say: *not my fault, M'lord!*

The inquiry had invited Andrew and Lisa to come and

give Saffie's pen portrait. They were supposed to sketch out her life, move the room to tears, then leave. The inquiry itself wanted Andrew to give them an advance script of what he was going to say for the pen portrait. But Andrew had refused. He had other things in mind. He was now Saffie's voice as well as his own. And he was aware the nation's media would be watching.

Lisa knew Andrew inside and out. And she knew that Andrew was never going to do what he was told. He was not intimidated by the inquiry, and he would do what he felt was right.

They checked into the Midland Hotel, a historic hotel in Manchester city centre, where the Conservative Party would often hold their annual political conferences. The hotel was where Charles Rolls met Henry Royce in 1904, a partnership which would become Rolls-Royce, one of the most famous car brands in the world.

In the afternoon, Andrew met with Nicola Brook, their solicitor. He wanted to visit the City Room in person before he gave evidence in the witness box. He wanted to see it with his own eyes.

"I think it would be a good idea if I came with you," Brook told him.

Andrew agreed, and so the two of them drove to the arena in Andrew's car and parked up.

It was the first time he had returned since the night of the bomb. He walked along Victoria Approach, pausing for a moment to look at the street corner, by the music school, where he had first found Ashlee, lying on the pavement, being helped by the trainee doctors.

He thought about those two young people who had stayed and helped when others had run away. He wondered where they were now, and how they were getting on at medical school. He felt grateful for everything they did for him and his family that night.

They entered Victoria train station and went up the stairs and over the walkway into the City Room. The doors leading into the arena were closed, but the City Room was open to walk around in.

Andrew was shocked. It was much smaller than he had expected. *How could Abedi have hidden in here for an hour?*

He walked up the stairs to the spot where Abedi had been sitting. He looked to where he knew Saffie had been, almost in the centre of the room, heading to the walkway.

He imagined her, holding her mother's hand, eyes shining, excited to find him outside and tell him about the concert. He didn't want to think about what happened next. It was too painful. Too raw.

In the corner of the room was a collection of flowers and cards for the victims. To this day in Manchester, the corner of that room contains flowers, cards and tributes to those who died. Manchester never forgets.

Andrew returned to the hotel feeling emotionally drained by the experience. Lisa didn't feel much like eating because she was so nervous about the next day. They bought some sandwiches in Tesco and took them to their rooms. It was almost time.

*

The next morning, Andrew left Lisa and Xander at the hotel with Lisa's close friend, Sam. Lisa's evidence would be played to the inquiry on a pre-recorded video, while Andrew was going to give evidence in person with Ashlee.

Andrew and Ashlee met with their legal team in a coffee shop before heading to Manchester Magistrates' Court.

"If it gets too overwhelming, just let them know and they can stop it and give you a break," Weatherby told them.

Weatherby was a calming presence. He was the right sort of person to have around you in such moments. Unsurprisingly, Andrew had never given evidence to a public inquiry before. Few members of the public have, so this was all new to him. Weatherby helped prepare him by describing the process and what he could expect from the day.

There would be another family giving their pen portrait first. Then Paul Greaney, the inquiry's barrister, would call on Andrew to stand and read out his pre-prepared words about Saffie. Andrew had those words on a piece of paper in the inside pocket of his suit jacket. The hotel receptionist had printed it off for him.

They headed for the courtroom, which can be found down a side street off Deansgate. Young professionals and office workers bustled past, coffee in hand, heading to work in one of the city's countless office complexes.

Manchester Magistrates' Court is an imposing building: modern looking, with a glass façade between brick columns, where the Royal coat of arms sits, featuring a lion and a unicorn prancing by a crown.

They were searched by security guards on the ground floor, passed through an airport-style scanner, then went up a long and high elevator which led up to the courtrooms.

The inquiry started at 9.30am. The first pen portrait to be heard that day was for Wendy Fawell, aged 50, from West Yorkshire. The mother-of-two had been waiting to collect her daughter in the City Room with her friend Caroline, when the bomb exploded.

At the end of the tributes, Sir John Saunders thanked the family for telling him about Wendy. "She was a larger than life figure," he said, "who gave so much to make the lives of others happy. Thank you."

At 11am, it was Saffie's turn.

"This is the pen portrait of Saffie-Rose Roussos, who I will call Saffie during the course of my introduction," Paul Greaney, counsel for the inquiry, said. "She was aged just eight years when she was killed and this pen portrait has been prepared by her family.

"In the hearing room alongside me are Saffie's dad, Andrew Roussos, and Saffie's sister, Ashlee Bromwich. Watching remotely are Saffie's mum, Lisa, who we will see in a short time pay tribute to her daughter in a video recording.

"Lisa will be with Xander, Lisa and Andrew's son, and the brother of Saffie. A family friend, Sam Harrison, will be there with them. Other family and friends will be watching from locations throughout the United Kingdom and in Cyprus ...

"Sir, I'm now going to invite Andrew, when he's ready, to stand and pay tribute to his daughter."

Andrew Roussos stood. He took a moment to pick up his reading glasses and put them on. "First, I would like to thank you, Sir, the inquiry team, and my legal team for their dedication towards our daughter, Saffie. Mr Greaney, we are watching the inquiry remotely and you are coming across with the highest compassion and sensitivity." He paused for a moment, took a deep breath, then started.

"My daughter, Saffie. How can I describe perfection? How do you describe heart melting love? How can I explain those big brown eyes? How can I stand here and explain to you all in words what a beautiful little girl she is?

"It's like the best artists got together and drew her from top to toe, with a heart so pure, so innocent she melted people's hearts. Her mum worried in this world that we live in about how open, trusting and social she is. I use 'she is' as I can't accept I'm doing this without Saffie. It's like having an out-of-body experience, it can't be real. That will never happen. I am never going to accept life without Saffie. She is my star, my admiration, my perfect daughter."

Going out with Saffie was like magic, he said. She captured people by looking at them and smiling. Andrew remembered how they would be stopped on the street by people commenting how beautiful she was with her eyes and smile. "She always made people laugh, filled them full of love, always wanted to stop and help people in need, and even then got a compliment and a smile," he said.

"Don't get me wrong, she had a naughty side that drove us up the wall. Five minutes before school, she used to put empty yoghurt pots in her brother Xander's shoes, stalling him getting out of the house so she could sit in the car where she liked.

"Laid-back Xander didn't know what hit him as she worked him to her advantage, but I remember the first time Xander had a sleepover, the back of the car was silent and when I looked back the tears were running down her face.

"Bravery and strength is one thing that she has. Just like her mum, she will fight to the end and not show defeat in anything she faced. From smashing the record on a pogo stick to climbing the highest, somersaulting in the most daring places. I've got to say, she kept us on our toes."

She was a free spirit, Andrew said. "We watched and protected. I used to try and calculate the dangers ahead that could occur as Saffie was skipping down the pavement without a care in the world."

The first night Saffie had a sleepover, Andrew had a panic attack, he remembered. "I remember waking at 3am ... worrying about what could happen as our friends might not fully understand how daring she could be. I wanted to go and fetch her so I could keep her safe, but at the same time, knew how disappointed Saffie would be as she was sleeping over for the first time."

Andrew said how much she loved gymnastics. "She would practice and practice until it was perfect," he said. "Mum and I took her to join a class because we were getting worried about these back flips and somersaults and jumping off walls would end up in disaster. On her first lesson her teacher said she needed to move to a more advanced class as she was special. I looked at Saffie and I said, 'Are you excited?' for her to reply, 'No.' I looked at her and said, 'Why?' 'I already know everything, daddy.'"

Saffie loved to explore and see new things, Andrew said. "She loved big cities, big cities of a night-time when all the lights were switched on. I remember the first time we all went to New York. I waited for dusk before I took her to Times Square. As we turned the corner I covered her eyes. What can I say? That look of amazement will stay with me, forever …

"I can go on and on. Never will there be another Saffie. Never will there be another kiss, a cuddle or a smile. I try and picture what she would look like now, what she would be doing. What career she would choose to the wedding dress she would pick to the adult Saffie would be … all she wanted to be is happy, loving and free to be a child, as every child should be."

Andrew finished. The room was silent for a moment.

"I'm now going to ask Ashlee, once she's ready, to stand, if she wishes to do so, and read her tribute to Saffie," said

Paul Greaney sombrely, looking a little affected by what he had just heard.

Ashlee stood up. Her hair was dark and sleek. She was dressed in black, with a gold necklace showing outside her top.

"Saffie-Rose, my sister, was the most beautiful and innocent little girl, yet very cheeky and mischievous in her own way. She would know exactly how to get just what she wanted with just one big huge beaming grin. It was impossible to ever say no.

"Her soul brought so much joy and energy. She would always be dancing, singing, spinning, doing acrobatics. She was a born entertainer. And I knew for the rest of her life she would live to put a smile on everybody's face, even a stranger's.

"She loved to make people laugh, usually by doing something ridiculously silly, and if she knew she could make you laugh the first time, she would never stop. And if you didn't laugh, she would never stop trying until she had you in the palm of her hand.

"The highlight of my week was visiting my family. Away from the troubles of the world, I knew they were always there to keep me going and keep life wholesome, being able to spend time with Saffie and my brother, Xander. Saffie would always ask me, 'Ashlee, can we play a game?' I'd never hear the end of it until I gave in and said yes."

She remembered surprising Xander and Saffie by picking them up from school. "I'd be waiting for them in the school playground, waiting for them to spot me. She'd come running over. 'What are you doing here?' And she would always ask, 'Have you got me anything?' usually meaning more sweets. So I learned my lesson never to arrive empty-handed when coming to see Saffie.

"I was always proud to call Saffie my sister. I still am. She was somebody I always wanted to tell people about and talk about. She was more than special: a rare soul. I didn't really ever realise just how precious each and every one of those times would be.

"How I wish I had said yes to every single time she would ask me to play a game with her. What I would give to see her running out of those school doors again, directly towards me. Our family will never be the same. Each and every one of us remains a spare part watching the world pass us by.

"I have lost the ability to feel such emotions other than grief and anger. It's like falling down a never-ending empty pit of sadness. We are here but not. Our bodies move and our voices can be heard, but our minds are absent. Still, we carry on the days for each other, my family. It doesn't get easier, just more and more confusing and the constant question of why.

"The things that once brought us joy don't. How can we feel joy in our lives without Saffie? She was our joy. The way I see the world will never be the same. I feel so naïve to think that life could bring no harm to those I love. Saffie didn't know the horrors of this world. A child should be allowed to live an innocent life. At eight years old she should only have known love and happiness and what she could only dream to become one day ...

"She won't get to meet my daughter, but I know she would have been the most loving, incredible aunt and role model. But my daughter will know her because we will never stop keeping her alive and taking her with us wherever we go.

"Thank you."

Chris, Andrew's brother, spoke in a pre-prepared video, along with his wife, Pat. Saffie was a character, he said. She was special. She could have been something spectacular. She would eat constantly.

Then Saffie's godmother appeared on the video. Saffie would call her Nouna, which means godmother in Greek. "One thing I will never forget is while I was baptising her, she didn't scream or cry, instead she was telling me to put on her baptising outfit."

Saffie's best friend from school came on the video, her face blurred so she could not be identified. "I took her to her first disco and she loved it, but before the disco we gave each other a face tattoo with red Sharpie, and it never came off, so we went to the school disco with big red blotches on our faces.

"When we went to her house we always used to sing and play the drums in the chippy, and the first thing she'd say to me when we got in the car was, 'I'm going to have a burger,' and she goes, 'because that's my favourite thing in the whole wide world.' Then I'd say, 'I'll have fish and chips because that's my favourite thing.'

"Our signature thing was when we were in bed and we had hot chocolate. We loved it. Her favourite song was 'One Last Time' by Ariana Grande and her favourite singer was Ariana Grande.

"When she's older, I reckon she would be a famous dancer. I don't know why, I could just tell. A normal day with Saffie would be crazy, but now a normal day to us is just calm, and I don't like it. I have dreams of Saffie, waiting for me at the school gate and wake up and it isn't real. I feel torn, I feel broken, and I just miss her so, so much."

Her friend's mother then spoke. "The funniest, the best sense of humour out of any eight-year-old I've ever met in my life. The biggest heart – oh, you've never heard a laugh like her."

She remembered her daughter telling her one day, "Mum, I want to go to heaven. I want to go to heaven and I want to be with her, I wish I went to the arena with her, so I was with her and I could push her out of the way."

She said her daughter felt guilty. "And every single day it's guilt," she said. "There's never a single day that goes by that Saffie isn't involved in our life. We've got pictures of her round the house, songs come on the radio, the radio gets switched off, my daughter can't process the songs. I don't know if she ever will."

Mike, from the computer shop, came on the video next. "She was lovely. Adorable. A pain in the arse."

Sam Harrison was next on the video. "Hi. My name is Sam and I'm a very close and dear friend to Lisa and Andrew, who I have known for around 25 years and I would like to share with you today some of my memories of Saffie-Rose."

She remembered Saffie being determined to dress herself. "I remember Lisa would leave clothes out for her in the morning to wear, which Saffie would completely ignore and bounce into the room in a completely different random and mismatched outfit. We'd just roll our eyes and laugh. Lisa would know she wouldn't win this argument.

"Our final memories of Saffie were a few weeks before the attack and we decided to go to the funfair. Saffie was fearless and wanted to go on everything. She also had a very special connection and bond with George (her son) so she spent most of the day with George going on all the rides, the faster the better."

Then Chloe, after that, who worked in the shop. She called Saffie "cheeky", "charming" and "confident. "A bit too confident sometimes with the fear factor being zero." She had imagined Saffie being her bridesmaid one day, aged 19. "I struggle to talk about what happened," Chloe said. "I struggle to look at any news posts, talk to people about it, look at photos ... It affected a few of my relationships and just general life, really."

The video then ran into a montage. Everglow played in the background, as videos and photographs were shown of Saffie. "You can't stop talking about Ariana Grande!"

Xander told her in one family video. A picture showed Saffie in a straw hat and sunglasses and a blue denim skirt; another picture of her cheek to cheek with Lisa, both beaming at the camera; another of her playing on the beach with Xander; then a video of her blowing into a trombone which was far too big for her. The montage came to an end.

Then Lisa appeared on the video, sitting on a chair against a blank white wall, her blonde hair in its typical fringe.

"Hi. I'm Lisa Roussos the proud mummy of beautiful Saffie-Rose. Saffie as a little girl was gentle and shy. But at the same time, she loved to be around people especially friends and family. She was a very helpful and pleasing little girl, who loved to dance and make people laugh.

"I remember taking Saffie to school on her first day. She was very excited now that she could go to school with her brother Xander. I left her playing happily as I walked away in tears. Later that day, as I walked to pick her up, her teacher spoke to me and informed me that Saffie had been playing dress-up and had lost a shoe. They had looked everywhere but couldn't find it, so she came home with one shoe. Saffie found it very funny.

"As Saffie grew, she became more confident and outgoing. She remained very gentle and helpful, always giving us cuddles and leaving little notes of 'I love you' everywhere. She looked up to big sister, Ashlee, and absolutely adored Xander.

"She was a sensitive soul who loved and gave generously.

She had a way with people, she could engage with them whoever they were. She could and would talk to people and have their complete attention, all the time being her gentle, funny self. She had this amazing, magnetic personality that drew people to her of all ages and I would just watch with wonder.

"I remember being in Croatia on holiday and we were staying in a local resort. We had a meal in the busy restaurant and Saffie wanted dessert. We looked over at the dessert table and there was a long queue. Saffie stood up and walked to the front of the queue. She looked up at the man behind her and gave him the biggest smile. She got the cake.

"She was special, and I understood this the moment she was born ... She was eight years old, yet she felt empathy and pain for others. She was clever and imaginative, bright and beautiful, funny and kind. She was enthusiastic about everything. She lit up any room and was so very precious."

Saffie didn't like people being sad and would do her best to make people laugh, Lisa said. She would never walk past a homeless person without giving them money and a smile.

"To say our lives now are completely devastated is an understatement," she said. "Saffie completed our family and was a huge part of it, the leader of it, you might say, always taking centre stage.

"The day I woke up from the coma, Andrew held my hand and looked up at me. I instantly knew. 'Saffie has gone, hasn't she?' Andrew nodded. I cried and begged and pleaded with him to let me die too. 'I can look after her,' I cried.

"I did die that day. Inside I'm dead. My heart is so heavy, it weighs me down. I've still got my part to play in my family. I'm a wife and a mother and I have to be there for Andrew, Ashlee and Xander. When my children are grown and have their own families and I have fulfilled my role as a mother, I'll be with my little Saffie, again."

Solicitors with years of experience looked upset in the room. So did some of the reporters in the annexe.

After watching Lisa, Andrew knew, in that moment, that he had to say something. He suddenly stood up. Paul Greaney looked over with curiosity, as did many in the room.

"Sir, could I just say something before I finish?" Andrew said to Sir John Saunders, the inquiry chairman.

Sir John looked up with a look of faint surprise. "Of course."

Andrew had prepared a speech. Even Pete Weatherby knew nothing about it.

Andrew cared nothing for the number of qualifications and reputations in the room. He was determined for Saffie's voice to be heard. That was what he cared about the most.

"I just feel I need to say a couple of words. Sir, with the highest respect I feel I need to say this ...

"What we are now going through, the failures we are all listening to, and the excuses we will all sit through needs to stop. Enough is enough, Sir. At present in 2020 if we are still learning lessons, then nothing will ever change. The biggest lesson and wake-up call should have come from 7/7 and 9/11. Saffie's life is not a practice exercise for the security services or the emergency services. Sir, lessons should already have been learnt and already in place.

"Sir, with the greatest respect, thank you."

"Thank you," Sir John said. "It's very difficult to say anything after those tributes. But can I say, thank you to Andrew and Ashlee for reading them, those moving tributes, and to all those on the video who have given equally moving tributes.

"Andrew, you described Saffie as your star, and from all we have heard, you were right to describe her that way: she was a star.

"Her death and the manner of it has been and still is devastating to her family and friends and we do understand that. Her star will continue to live in your hearts. For the rest of us, the star that was Saffie has stopped, and we are all the losers for it."

Chapter 24
Saving Saffie

It was New Year when Pete Weatherby received a 23-page medical report commissioned by the inquiry to look at how Saffie died on the night of the bomb. The report was a second opinion and its findings were incendiary. He read the report, read it again, then sat back at his desk in his home in Manchester.

It was hard reading. He knew what its findings would mean to Andrew and Lisa. He knew the bombshell it was going to drop on the public inquiry. He discussed the findings with Nicola Brook and Elkan Abrahamson, the solicitors who had instructed him.

In essence, the findings were clear: Saffie could have and should have been saved. But the report came into direct conflict with the findings of the inquiry's own blast wave panel.

In order to examine the case of each individual who had died, so that the inquiry's chairman, Sir John Saunders, could decide if more could have been done to save them, a blast wave panel had been commissioned to investigate. The experts on that panel were made up of a bioengineering professor at Imperial College; three colonels in the British Army, one a surgeon, the other a consultant radiologist, the third a professor at the Royal Centre of Defence medicine;

and an engineer from Porton Down, the government's secret research laboratory.

They had looked at the witness statements, medical paperwork and scans, and any other evidence, as they considered the most important question for any of the families: could their loved one have been saved?

Of the 22 who died, three were pronounced dead in hospital. Those were John Atkinson, Georgina Callander, and Saffie.

At the start of the inquiry, only Atkinson's injuries were considered to have been potentially "survivable", according to the blast wave experts. Atkinson, who was 28, lay bleeding in the City Room for up to 50 minutes, during which time he told a police officer: "I'm gonna die." He was carried on a makeshift stretcher to a casualty clearing area and later suffered a cardiac arrest one hour and 16 minutes after the blast.

In Saffie's case, the blast wave panel had effectively changed their minds on whether or not she could survive. Their first report had said she was "unlikely" to survive because of her injuries, but it was possible. In other words: she had a chance.

But in March 2020, an addendum to the original report changed that opinion. It now concluded that Saffie's injuries were unsurvivable with current advanced medical treatment. To Lisa, that was like mental torture, first being told she could have lived, then being told she could not. Which was it?

Weatherby was deeply unimpressed with the lack of consistency shown by the blast wave panel, and the fact they had changed their opinion so substantially. After all, this was no small matter for the Roussos family. This was the difference between life and death.

He informed Sir John that Andrew and Lisa were unhappy with the blast wave panel's change in their conclusions and they would like a second opinion. Sir John, a fair-minded judge who realised that, first and foremost, the public inquiry was about the families getting the truth about how their loved ones died, agreed.

The two experts approached by the inquiry for a second opinion were Lieutenant Colonel Claire Park, a consultant in intensive care and pre-hospital care, and Dr Gareth Davies, a consultant in emergency medicine and pre-hospital care. Both of them had hands-on experience of jumping out of helicopters and dealing with people in dire need of emergency treatment. Park had served in Iraq and Afghanistan and had over 20 years of deployed military experience. She had provided front-line care in battlefields to soldiers who had suffered from blast explosions. Davies, meanwhile, had spent much of his career as medical director at London's Air Ambulance and had attended many disaster scenes, including the London bombings of 7 July, 2005.

They had looked at the same evidence as the blast wave panel and decided that Saffie could have been saved. And it was Weatherby's job to deliver the devastating news to her parents.

*

A few days later, on 18 January, 2021, Paul Greaney stood behind his desk in an empty room at the Manchester Arena Inquiry.

"Sir, I'm told you've joined us, but we can't see you," he told Sir John Saunders.

"Can you see me now?" Sir John asked.

"Sir, I can see you."

Sir John's face appeared on a screen. He was on his computer at home, smartly dressed in a dark suit, white shirt and light blue tie, with framed pictures on shelves in the background. "Have the technical difficulties been overcome ...?

Greaney confirmed they had.

Sir John explained that he was joining remotely because he had not yet received his Covid-19 vaccination. He explained he was in one of the vulnerable categories and did not want to risk catching the coronavirus and causing delays for the inquiry.

The public inquiry had reached an important stage. It was going to consider the response of the emergency services, and how they had performed on the night of the arena bomb. The survivors inside the City Room had reported a delay in receiving help and for some, that delay had been fatal. Others, like Lisa herself, had lost a huge amount of blood from lying on the floor of the City Room without medical attention, and were lucky to survive.

There had been only one paramedic inside the room in the first three quarters of an hour after the bomb, and only three paramedics would ever enter. The rest would remain outside due to safety fears.

The fire brigade, which had vital medical equipment and stretchers which could have been used to carry out the survivors, took more than two hours to arrive. The rescue service had managed to rescue not one person on the night of the arena bomb. Fire chiefs had kept their engines away in case their firefighters got hurt by a terrorist.

Paul Greaney then raised the issue of survivability. As mentioned earlier, the blast wave panel considered John Atkinson to have sustained injuries which should have been "survivable", meaning he might have lived had he been given better emergency treatment.

But what about Saffie?

By now the inquiry had received the second-opinion report. This was an important moment for Andrew and Lisa and their legal team. Was the inquiry going to accept the findings?

Was it going to accept that there was doubt over the findings of the blast wave panel of experts?

"The blast wave experts characterised Saffie as being unlikely to survive her injuries, but they did not say that they were certainly unsurvivable," Greaney said. "However, in an addendum report dated in March of last year, prepared following the consideration of further material, the blast wave experts concluded that Saffie's injuries were unsurvivable with current advanced medical treatment."

Greaney paused. "Evidence has, however, been received by the inquiry from additional experts. That evidence has been received via the family of Saffie, although the inquiry legal team was consulted.

"The experts that we've just referred to are Dr Gareth Davies and Lieutenant Colonel Claire Park. They observe Saffie sustained serious injuries to her chest, abdomen and legs. She was, they observed, tended to by members of the public, first-aiders, police and ambulance staff who recognised the seriousness of Saffie's injuries and cared for her with compassion and a clear desire to help save her life.

"Ultimately, the experts conclude, blood loss from the injuries to Saffie's legs eventually led to her heart stopping and her death. These experts consider that the injuries in isolation or in combination, although severe, did not reach a threshold where they would be considered incompatible with life ... and so they consider that Saffie may have survived."

Greaney explained what must happen now. "These experts and the blast wave experts will meet in order to identify areas of agreement and disagreement, if any, in order to assist the chairman when he hears evidence on this issue."

The inquiry would listen to the findings of the second opinion. The new evidence would be admitted.

The truth would be heard, Andrew and Lisa thought.

Chapter 25
The Lost Hours

Throughout 2021, the inquiry heard witnesses from the police, fire and rescue and ambulance services. A picture was emerging of survivors being left to bleed in the City Room as police officers begged for assistance from paramedics who were not coming inside to help. Those officers on the ground did their best to save lives, without the necessary skills or equipment. There were people in the room whose conduct that night was nothing short of heroic.

Inspector Mike Smith, one of the first unarmed officers to arrive in the room after the bomb, took charge as best he could, and directed his officers to carry survivors out of the room to where they could find the paramedics. He could be heard on his radio repeatedly asking for paramedics to come inside, knowing the room was safe.

There was no armed terrorist in the room, or secondary device. Smith could see that after a few minutes of arriving. Just a lot of people, dying in front of his very eyes.

Paul Reid, a poster seller, was also inside the room. He stayed with Saffie until she was taken away in an ambulance. He could have chosen to run away, like so many did. Instead he chose to stay. In an interview with the media months later, he described still being able to hear the sound of the alarms going off in the room when he went to sleep at night; the smell of smoke, and the feeling of panic.

There was Darron Coster, a retired military police officer, who ran inside the room after the explosion, using a belt and a handbag strap as tourniquets. Coster would die four years later in a head-on crash with a car in North Yorkshire while riding his motorbike.

Sir John, the inquiry chairman, used the word "hero" to describe Coster's actions that night, using his military training to save lives, even having the awareness to close the doors to the room to protect onlookers from the trauma of what was inside.

The first three British Transport Police (BTP) officers entered the City Room fewer than two minutes after the explosion, among them one officer who had been on a kebab break. After the bomb exploded, she showed great courage to enter the room and report what she could see and hear. The lights in the City Room were still on and there were many casualties.

Three minutes after the explosion four BTP officers were in the room; seven minutes after the explosion, nine officers were in the room or on the raised walkway into the room. They were quickly joined by officers from Greater Manchester Police (GMP).

But where were the paramedics and the fire and rescue service? Why did they not flood the room after the bomb? And why were the police officers in the room forced to use metal railings and advertising boards as stretchers to get people out?

*

The inquiry pieced together what happened inside the City Room that night by speaking to witnesses who were present, looking at CCTV footage, and examining footage from police body-worn cameras.

On 12 May, 2022, Inspector Mike Smith came to the inquiry to give his evidence about what happened. Smith had joined Greater Manchester Police in 1992 and trained as a detective constable, then a response and custody sergeant. He was promoted to inspector and had experience of taking charge of many different crime scenes: murders, serious traffic collisions, suicides, and fatal tram collisions. But he had never seen anything like the night of the bomb. Few people have.

He was in uniform that night and coming into Central Park Police Station – about two miles north of the arena – when the bomb exploded.

Smith was radioed at 10.34pm. "Go ahead," he said.

"Urgent. Explosion at the foyer by the old McDonald's at Manchester Arena, upwards of 30 to 40 people injured," said the police radio operator.

Smith checked on the police computer system and quickly read the reports coming in from members of the public.

People who call 999 speak to a control room operator. Their call will be typed up and logged as an incident report, which goes into a system which Smith could see. There were too many reports coming in from members of the public for it to be a hoax. This had to be real.

He grabbed one of his sergeants and in two minutes flat they were in a police car speeding with flashing blue lights to Victoria Railway Station.

"Where do you want the RVP, boss?" asked the radio operator. RVP was short for rendezvous point – where the emergency services could meet up to organise their response.

Smith thought for a moment. He had worked in the city centre for some time and knew the area. "The cathedral ... there's a parking area outside the cathedral."

He instructed any officers to head directly to Victoria Station itself. He also told control to let the night silver commander know what was going on at the arena. The silver commander would be the person who had tactical control of the terror attack.

That night, the silver commander was Superintendent Arif Nawaz, one of the City of Manchester superintendents.

At 10.44pm, Smith arrived on Station Approach. He had managed to get to the scene with incredible speed. It was hardly 10 minutes since he had been informed a bomb had gone off.

The arena would normally fall to the responsibility of BTP, being right next to a major train station. But this was a terror attack. The incident had to be under GMP control, and that made him bronze commander, meaning he had operational command on the ground.

Smith checked on a couple of injured casualties outside the station, then assigned officers to close off the roads around the arena, using the radio on his body armour. He knew the emergency services would need space to work.

He entered the train station. "BTP are inside," he said on his radio to the control room. "They're saying the major casualties are inside. I'm just going to track them down now."

He came across a group of firearms officers in the station concourse, in front of the walkway to the City Room. They were wearing their ballistic helmets. They were searching the station and the arena complex, making it safe.

At 10.48pm, Smith entered the room.

"I think it was quite clear to me straightaway, really, that there had been an explosion," Smith told the inquiry, "that there were some badly injured people there, and we needed a strategy for how we were going to deal with those.

"I do remember walking round the room, probably trying to think about what to do to get a grip of this, really, and I think my strategy from a pretty early stage was: we need to get the people who are injured out of here, longer term this is a crime scene, it will need sealing, if you like, and then looking at the sort of resources we would need to get those people out of the room."

"What was your immediate priority?" asked Nicholas de la Poer, one of the barristers for the inquiry's legal team.

"Preservation of life, the people who were injured," Smith said.

Smith conducted a risk assessment as soon as he entered, and his evidence was vital for understanding why he believed the City Room was safe for the fire service and the paramedics to flood the zone and help the critically injured.

"I think I could see that a bomb had gone off. I could see, I think, where the seat of the explosion had been," Smith told the inquiry. "Then I needed to decide if it was safe or safe enough for me and for everybody else to be there.

"I did decide that I couldn't rule out the fact that there may be other attackers or terrorists within the complex, but I was pretty happy there were no other terrorists within the City Room itself.

"The rest of the complex, the arena is obviously quite a large building, I couldn't rule that out. I could see that there were some firearms officers present already, I was aware I'd seen a couple coming in who were kitted up, ready to go. My guess was that there would be more and more coming, so I felt safe in that scene from a firearms attack of any kind.

"There was nothing over the air to me suggesting that there was anybody roaming with a weapon. I've mentioned before about the only hint of gunfire was quickly ruled out so far as I was concerned. I couldn't rule out the fact that there might have been a secondary device there, but I think the rapid conclusion I came to was that it was unlikely."

Smith had firearms training and training as a police search adviser, part of which is a joint military and police training programme, which had given him awareness of terrorist methods of attack.

He could clearly see the attack was the result of one man who had blown himself up in roughly the centre of the room. That individual was well and truly dead.

After a few minutes of looking around the room, he stepped aside and got on the radio. "It looks to me like a bomb's gone off, here. I would say there's about 30 casualties. Could you have every available ambulance to me, please?"

The bronze commander was asking for every available paramedic to come to him that very instant.

BTP constables Matthew Martin and Carl Roach had also arrived in the room. Martin was a clean-cut young officer. A few minutes earlier he had been chasing a bike thief across town when he was contacted by his control room to say there had been an explosion at the arena.

The City Room was a mess. People inside were running in different directions, panicking. There was shouting and screaming. People were on the floor covered in blood. A burning smell lingered in the air.

Smith was in direct charge of a small group of GMP officers and BTP officers, who were working with arena staff and Emergency Training UK (ETUK) personnel, a first aid company hired by the arena operators for the night of the concert. The injuries they were suddenly faced with went well beyond their expertise.

The officers were getting more and more frustrated. They needed help.

"We need paramedics like fucking yesterday," shouted one of the officers on the radio.

At 10.50pm, Smith had a conversation with a radio operator based in the control room alongside the force duty officer (FDO) – a police inspector who at that exact moment was in overall charge of the emergency service response. The FDO was the boss until a proper command structure could be put in place.

"I need every North West Ambulance Service (NWAS) facility that we've got in here, please, directly in here," he told the operator.

Sir John Saunders interrupted his evidence at the inquiry with a question: "And you wouldn't have said that unless you were satisfied as you could be in your own mind that it was safe for them to come in there?"

"Safe enough, sir," Smith said.

He ordered a sergeant to go and make sure the station was sealed off to members of the public. He told that sergeant: "Just make sure the ambulance, any ambulance, come in. Get them straight up."

Smith estimated there were around 10 unarmed police officers in the room, trying to help. That number later got up to around 30, in and around the City Room on the night, he said.

At 10.51pm, Smith spoke to his officers on the radio. "Send one of the PCs outside to tell any NWAS staff they need to get in here as soon as."

Smith ran out onto the walkway outside the City Room

where he found Patrick Ennis, an advanced paramedic. They walked back inside the room together. At 10.52pm, Ennis was the first paramedic to enter. The ambulances were piling up outside, but nobody was coming into the room to help. Their bosses had concerns about more attacks from terrorists and held them back. Ennis told Smith the plan was to set up a casualty station on the station concourse below.

Smith said more paramedics should come to the City Room. They had people who were dead and dying. The survivors were bleeding to death, right in front of his officers.

Where were the paramedics?

Smith got back on the radio to his control room. "Paramedic has just arrived now. He's just having a look round to assess but still if we get any more NWAS resources, send them in as soon as, please."

The situation was desperate. It was at that moment GMP's Tactical Aid Unit, led by Sergeant Kam Hare, arrived in the room. Smith felt a moment of relief. *Thank God.* Smith knew Hare. The unit were the very best of GMP, known within the force as the "can-do" team. And they were needed now, more than ever.

At 10.55pm, Smith gave an instruction to Sergeant Hare. "If they are obviously dead, just leave them."

Smith explained what he meant by that to the inquiry. "Our role there was really to preserve life. It sounds very harsh and cold to say that, but what I wanted the officers there to concentrate on was the living and getting them to a position where they could be given potentially life-saving care and treatment."

Hare directed his team to work in pairs and administer first aid. He reassured his officers that paramedics were on their way. His officers did all they could, but they did not have the training of paramedics. They had their limitations.

At 10.56pm, Smith was back on to his control room. "At the minute the only NWAS unit who's here is (Ennis) ... so any others that arrive, you can direct them in here again, please."

The radio messages were being given on an open radio channel, meaning that police officers with radios in the area could pick up Smith's repeated requests for paramedics.

Smith was passed a report from a member of the public which had come through a BTP sergeant. An Asian male had been seen by a member of the public putting down a rucksack and running away. The person was wearing glasses, a cap, and had a large black rucksack. Smith reported it to the control room. The report turned out to be bogus.

The control room then piped up. "I've got you 11 ambulances en route," said the radio operator.

"Are they coming to the front entrance?" Smith said. "Can I give you an update as well? I think we may well have found our bomber. He's very dead."

The paramedics set up a casualty clearing station by the exit of the train station. The paramedic commander on the ground had decided that non-specialist paramedics should not be deployed into the City Room. He believed that he was prohibited from deploying those paramedics into the room.

By 11.11pm, Smith assessed that around 15 people had died. He was now giving instructions to his officers to get people out of the room on improvised stretchers. Metal crash barriers, advertising hoardings, whatever it took.

Around this time Ennis had returned to the room after leaving to report back to the paramedic commander about the state of the survivors. He had not been asked to go back in, he had done so of his own accord to start doing triage. He thought paramedics would arrive behind him in swarms. He was wrong. Smith was having to make do with what he had.

"You were obviously faced with a very difficult situation ..." said de la Poer. "And so far as you could see, there were no stretchers, i.e. items designed for that purpose, readily at hand?"

"No," said Smith.

"There were items that could be used to improvise?"

"Yes."

"And there were undoubtedly people who would not be able to move themselves or even be assisted on their feet?"

"Yes."

The paramedics were not coming up to the room, but the casualty clearing station was across the walkway bridge, down the stairs, across the concourse and by the exit to the train station.

"My view was, well, we need to get them out as quickly

as possible and we'll use whatever we can to do that," Smith told the inquiry.

By now it was 11.17pm, and Smith's frustrations about the lack of paramedics in the room were clear. "We need more paramedics," one of his sergeants told him. "We need them in here now."

"They have a casualty clearing area out there which is fine but we need them in here," Smith said to his sergeant.

Smith ordered one of the BTP officers to physically go and get some paramedics to come into the room. He could see two survivors slipping away in front of his very eyes. They needed paramedics – now. The survivors' injuries were way beyond the capabilities of the first aid skills of his officers and the others in the room.

Two more paramedics arrived, making it three paramedics. They were from the ambulance service's Hazardous Area Response Team (HART), and wore distinctive green helmets. They had two six-person crews on duty that night. Only two paramedics arrived.

It wasn't enough. Not by a long shot. Smith wanted a pair of paramedics for each survivor who could move. Three paramedics was not going to work.

It took more than an hour for the last casualty to be taken out of the City Room. Lisa was the second last survivor to be carried out.

That hour, to Smith, did not seem like an hour. "I think the whole thing – it's probably the most intense hour, hour and a half of my life, certainly professional life."

"I hope it remains that way, too," Sir John said.

Smith shook his head. "I do too, sir."

At 11.47pm, Smith told the control room: "All the injured are out of the booking hall, now."

Smith stayed on duty and remained in the arena until 5am the next day. He went back to his police station and stayed there until he finished his shift, slightly before 7am.

"I think that's reasonable!" Sir John said.

"Thank you, Sir."

Those moments were the most challenging, traumatic and haunting of Smith's career. He experienced first-hand the actions of police officers, paramedics and members of the public who had worked together as a team to do their very best. "I am proud to have been part of that team effort," he told the inquiry.

He was proud of the efforts of his officers on the ground and in the City Room. But there were clearly serious problems with the emergency response raised by Smith's own evidence.

Smith could see with his own eyes there was no terrorist running around with a gun, or a secondary device. He had asked for paramedics to come into the room – again, and again, and again. What more could he do?

In the words of the final report made by the inquiry chair, Sir John Saunders, he had "performed admirably under great pressure".

But there was something Smith did not know that night. In a location some distance away, the force duty officer, the person in the police control room in overall charge of the response, had made a very important decision. He had called Operation Plato. And it would have devastating implications for the survivors in that room.

*

In Dorset, Andrew and Lisa had bought a new house. They knew they could not rent forever. They needed a house of their own which would give them long-term stability, in part because Xander had almost finished high school.

Lisa was browsing on a property website one day when she came across a bungalow in a village not far from the sea. It was a 1970s house tucked away in a cul-de-sac, with a nice sized garden at the front and back. There was plenty of space for a couple of cars on the drive, and the driveway was open and level, so that Lisa would be able to walk out of the house and into a car easily enough.

A house built on a slope would not work. Lisa's balance was not good. And going up and down stairs remained very painful, which was why it had to be a bungalow. It had two bedrooms and they wanted to have a look around to see if it could be converted into three bedrooms. One for them, one for Xander, the third for Saffie. They would always keep a room for Saffie. They would never move into a house where they could not have a room for her with all of her things.

The estate agent showed them inside. The house would

need to be stripped back and gutted. It had belonged to an elderly person, and had flowery carpets and curtains, maroon walls, mahogany furniture, and old-fashioned storage heaters.

There was an L-shaped lounge and a separate kitchen which Andrew thought they could knock through and make open-plan. There were two bedrooms and a third room being used as a study. The study had a nice view into the garden, where an apple tree grew to the side of the lawn, with deep flower beds.

They would have just about enough, combining money from selling their business in Leyland, with the money released to the family by the Manchester Fund. They made an offer, and a few days later were told their bid had been accepted.

They were mid-way through renovating when Inspector Smith gave his evidence to the inquiry. Andrew was struck by his bravery. Smith had tried his best in the worst situation ever. He didn't shirk his responsibilities, he took command on the night, and then he went to the inquiry and told the truth.

The City Room was safe for the paramedics to come inside, Smith had said. There was no reason to hold back the paramedics and firefighters. This had been a failure of communication.

Andrew drove to the new bungalow. The house was like a building site. They were still renting their other house and living there until the renovations had been complete. He stood in front of a large chimney breast which needed to come down.

He picked up a sledgehammer, and used his brute force to pound it down, brick for brick, not stopping until it had crumbled under the force of his rage.

Smith's words rang in his head, over and over again: every available ambulance to me, please.

Saffie could have been saved.

Chapter 26
"What's Operation Plato?"

A burly man with broad shoulders and a strong northern accent stepped into the witness box wearing a police uniform with three silver pips on each shoulder.

It was 5 May, 2021 and the UK was fighting against the spread of Covid-19. A one-metre social distancing rule was in place, indoor hospitality was closed, and funerals had a 30-person limit.

A middle-aged female court assistant in a black robe and face mask approached the box and held out a bible wrapped in a plastic bag.

"Can you repeat after me, please?" she said. 'I swear by almighty God ..."

"I swear by almighty God ..." the man responded.

"That the evidence I shall give ..."

"That the evidence I shall give ..."

"Shall be the truth ..."

"Shall be the truth ..."

"The whole truth ..."

"The whole truth ..."

"And nothing but the truth ..."

"And nothing but the truth ..."

The police officer took his seat.

Paul Greaney, counsel to the inquiry, stood at his desk

with his notes in front of him. This was a big moment for the families of those who had died in the bomb. "Would you begin by telling us your full name please?" Greaney asked.

"Dale John Sexton."

"Are you a chief inspector with Greater Manchester Police?"

"I am a chief inspector, yes, that's correct."

"Do you currently work as a force critical incident manager within specialist operations?"

"That's correct."

"Based at force headquarters?"

"Yes."

Sexton was the force duty officer, otherwise known as the FDO, on the night of the attack. The role of FDO is a highly demanding one. It usually meant managing the day to day business of the force, something which became even more important when the chiefs went home for the day. They were also in initial command of major incidents until a proper command team can be assembled.

Sexton had been a police officer for 30 years, joining in January 1991. He first worked in Rochdale, then was promoted to sergeant and transferred to the city centre. In 2001 he took his inspector's exams and was promoted again, working as a response inspector, dealing with 999 emergency call outs. After that he held a number of jobs in the force, working at one point for Ian Hopkins, when Hopkins was an assistant Chief Constable.

In 2014 Sexton applied for a vacancy which came up

within the force duty officer (FDO) cohort. He was attracted to it because it was a role where critical decisions had to be made.

An FDO is a sort of jack of all trades in the police force. They are regarded as somebody who knows everything, and if required can command all force resources. They are the "go-to" person for the force. The general rule was that if you don't know the answer to something, ask the FDO.

The job meant dealing and liaising on a regular basis with the fire and rescue service and ambulance service, making decisions on where to deploy aircraft and helicopters, and dealing with specialist resources, such as turning out mountain rescue for missing persons.

There was no formal course to complete to do the job. The only training possible was simply sitting next to an experienced FDO who could pass on their knowledge. It was not unheard of to be mentored for up to six months before being trusted to do the job on your own.

Sexton was the person inside the control room on the night of the bomb, in charge of organising the emergency services response. He was the boss, the person who called the shots, until the senior commanders could be raised and brought into headquarters.

The inquiry was able to piece together his actions that night using the incident log, witness testimony, transcripts of radio conversations, and Sexton's own electronic voice recorder.

Sexton's shift started quietly enough. There was little to

deal with, apart from the pursuit of a potentially stolen car. Then at 10.31pm, the bomb exploded in the City Room. Fifty-two seconds later, police received their first 999 call, from a member of the public called Ronald Blake. Minutes later three British Transport Police officers ran into the City Room. "It's definitely a bomb, people injured, at least 20 casualties," an officer told her control room.

At 10.34pm, Inspector Dale Sexton took command. He was an inspector at the time and was promoted to chief inspector by the force after the attack.

Sexton said he thought the bomb was a hoax, at first, then saw there were too many reports coming in. It had to be real. Paul Lawton, the police firearms tactical advisor that night, called him up. "Hiya boss, it's Paul Lawton," he said.

"It's looking legit this one," Sexton said.

"What is it, an explosion or gunshots?"

"An explosion reported and reports of gunshots," Sexton said. "I'm not too sure about the gunshots, but it's been reported as gunshots ... obviously we're going to have to get there and get in as quickly as possible."

"Straight to the scene?" Lawton said.

"Straight to the scene," Sexton said.

"Emergency search?"

"Yeah."

At 10.39pm, the force duty supervisor, Ian Randall, who was Sexton's number two, called Superintendent Nawaz to tell him about the explosion. Nawaz was the duty silver commander, meaning he would have tactical command.

"Hiya boss, it's Ian, one of the force duty supervisors, you know, the FDO's bagman."

"Oh, yes, yes," Nawaz said.

"We've had an explosion at Manchester ... Boss, are you near a box?" A box, in this context, meant a computer with access to the police incident log.

"I'm not," Nawaz said.

"We've had reports of an explosion in the foyer at the Manchester Arena where the old McDonald's was, you know at the main concourse? Everyone and his mam are going down there," Randall said.

"We're waiting for an update as soon as possible but it says at the minute about 20 to 30 people injured ... There's a concert on at the arena, would you believe?"

Randall said he would get a command module set up. This was where the commanders would work from, organising the response.

There are three levels of police commander for a major incident: bronze commander, which is operational and on the ground. This was Inspector Mike Smith. Silver commander, which is tactical. This was Superintendent Nawaz. And gold commander, which is strategic, who was Assistant Chief Constable Debbie Ford.

Dale Sexton, as FDO, was supposed to do the job of silver and gold commander until the team was set up. He was also supposed to organise the firearms teams on the ground.

At 10.39pm, PC Edward Richardson, the firearms commander on the ground, radioed the control room to say he and his team were outside the arena. They had managed to get there in eight minutes flat from the point the bomb went off.

One of the team, firearms officer Lee Moore, radioed the control room. "I'm going to the upper floor of the arena," he said. "They've got major casualties."

"Received," Sexton said over the radio. "Definitely casualties."

Lee Moore raised the possibility it might be an Operation Plato scenario. Plato was a very specific type of operation designed by the government and police to combat a marauding terrorist firearms attack – in other words, a terrorist who was shooting people.

Plato should only be called and kept in operation if a gunman is known to be in the area. This is because it creates a "no go" zone where the gunman is shooting people. Emergency services are ordered to stay back from the area to limit the body count, meaning those already injured in the "no go" zone, otherwise known as the "hot zone", are left to fight for themselves.

Because of the very obvious impact on survivors, Plato must be kept under constant review, and a hot zone must be lifted if it becomes clear there is no gunman in it.

At 10.43pm, Sexton was being updated by the two firearms officers on the ground, Richardson and Moore.

"Just confirm what you've heard, please?" Richardson asked Moore over the radio.

"I'm with a BTP officer now," Moore said. "We're going

up to the upper floor of the MEN (arena). It's stated that they've got major casualties upstairs in the MEN and they believe it's a ball bearing device. Stand by further."

"Yeah, received," Sexton said.

"Boss, I can confirm there's definitely casualties," Moore said a few seconds later.

"Yeah received, definitely casualties."

"Boss, confirmed. Yes, yes. Operation Plato, Operation Plato," Moore said.

Moore had no authority to call such an operation. Only Sexton could call Plato.

"What was happening in this conversation?" Paul Greaney, counsel to the inquiry, asked Sexton.

"I suppose it's a very, very quick way of saying, 'Boss, the circumstances justify Operation Plato.' It's not his decision, but it's a quick way for him to inform me of his concerns ..."

But Sexton never asked if there was evidence of an active shooter at the arena.

At 10.43pm a third armed response vehicle arrived at the arena. Substantial numbers of GMP armed police officers had arrived just minutes after the terror attack to secure Manchester.

By 10.44pm the firearms officers had been through the City Room and were now inside the arena, hunting for terrorists.

Greaney questioned Sexton about it.

" ... so within 14 minutes of the explosion, there have

actually been armed officers within that City Room – and not just within it, they've been through it?" Greaney said.

"Yes," Sexton responded in the witness box.

"Would it be fair to say that if by that stage there had been an active shooter within the City Room, you would have expected the armed police to have noticed or for some other person within the City Room to have drawn it to their attention?" Greaney asked.

Sexton said it was possible a terrorist could be in hiding, ready to pop out and start shooting. By this time the armed police had already done a thorough check of the room, checking every inch.

Back in the control room, Sexton could be heard having another conversation with PC Eddie Richardson, the firearms commander, who was giving him a briefing.

"At the moment we've got a large number of casualties inside the entrance to the arena, some are not in a good way," Richardson told him over the radio. "We've got paramedics and people administering first aid. We've got to consider also a secondary device. We've got no-one else coming forward in relation to being involved in this ..."

No-one else. The armed police had been through the City Room and seen no gunman inside.

Inspector Smith had arrived and was physically inside the City Room and could see there was no gunman inside.

British Transport Police were inside the City Room and could see there was no gunman inside.

At 10.47pm, Sexton declared Operation Plato, the

operation to stop a gunman on the loose. The City Room was made a "hot zone" which meant paramedics and firefighters would have to stay away, because there was a terrorist with a gun on the loose.

Except, there was no shooter. Just people dying.

The inquiry would eventually rule that Sexton had acted reasonably in his decision to first call Plato. He had an early report of gunfire from a member of the public. It was false, but he didn't know that. But the inquiry would also rule that by 10.50pm the City Room was in fact a cold zone. There was no threat from a terrorist with a gun inside the room. Only injured people who desperately needed medical inventions.

At 10.50pm, Superintendent Arif Nawaz, the silver commander in tactical command of the terror attack, called up. He wanted an update. "Dale, it's Arif. Sorry, just very quickly, we've got confirmed 10 dead with multiple injuries to other people, significant numbers, still trying to make sure that there's no further devices inside."

"Yeah," Sexton said.

" ... I'm going to have to pull in resources from other divisions."

"Yes," Sexton said. "I'm bringing in some ARVs (armed response vehicles) across from the airport and that's pretty much what we've got at the moment."

"I've just printed off the evacuation plan. I take it you've got that, have you?" Nawaz said.

"Boss, I haven't had a chance to look at the evacuation plan, I'm just dealing with what we've got at the moment."

Nawaz changed the conversation. "Right, so it's confirmed 10 dead at the location?"

"Confirmed 10 dead at the location, yes," Sexton said. " … It looks like there's been a male who's had a device strapped to him and exploded it … Ball bearings, et cetera. So I have declared an Op Plato, which is a terrorist attack."

"Op what?" Nawaz asked.

"Op Plato, which is a terrorist attack."

"Yeah."

"Ok? And obviously on the face of it at the moment we've only got one individual, a lone terrorist, but I've got to bear this in mind, that it might escalate even further."

It was a quite extraordinary exchange. Nawaz, the person who would be in tactical command of Operation Plato, appeared to have no idea what Operation Plato was.

Greaney pointed out that in order to be in charge of the tactical plan for Operation Plato that it might in fact to useful to know what it was in the first place.

Sexton agreed.

Nawaz was relieved of the role later that night and replaced by somebody else.

Sexton's phone was constantly going off. His dedicated phone line was jam packed, meaning many people could not get through. At just before 11pm, Sexton told a radio operator to come and start answering his phone, which was constantly ringing.

"Right, I want one of you down there to come up here, please, to answer my phone for me …" he ordered.

There was a limited number of phone lines into Sexton. They were being clogged up by calls from the media and others from around the force who wanted an update. The people he really needed to speak to were not getting through. The fire and rescue liaison tried seven times to get through to Sexton but his line was jammed.

There was no radio channel set up for police, fire and ambulance control rooms to communicate, leading to a complete breakdown in communication.

It was now 11.04pm. "Anyone who's walking wounded to be extracted out of the venue," Richardson said over the radio. "We've got a number of staff here who are – obviously they're not first aid trained but they're doing the best they can.

"If you can get anyone who can come in and basically extract anyone who can stand up and walk?"

Sexton said he did not give his full attention to Richardson's plea to extract the walking wounded. "I knew that we had lots of paramedics at the scene," he told the inquiry. "I wasn't aware that we only had a few paramedics inside the room."

"Boss, do you want media enquiries cancelling or do you want me to answer them?" asked the radio operator.

"No, I don't want you to speak to them at all," Sexton said, "I want you to tell them that we're too busy, they're going to have to wait. We've just turned out the media officer who should be able to start fielding those questions."

It was 11.12pm. Randall was about to leave to set up the command module for the police commanders. "Right, just give me a quick overview?" Randall asked Sexton.

"Quick overview," Sexton said. "We've got multiple fatalities, multiple casualties. We are trying to put a sterile cordon area around the MEN (arena). I am bringing in ARVs (armed response vehicles) from neighbouring forces, moving ARVs from other forces to our border area should we need to utilise them.

"I've declared Op Plato which is a marauding – which is a terrorist attack. I'm just speaking to military assets now to update them. Everyone knows who needs to know about it. I am satisfied, reasonably satisfied, that it was a lone actor on this one and therefore the priority now is for the casualties."

Sexton had updated his number two before he went to set up the module for the commanders. "Everybody knows who needs to know about it," he said.

But what about ambulance and fire and rescue?

Sexton had not contacted either of them. The person in charge of the emergency services response had not contacted the other emergency services. The response was not working together.

Paramedics and firefighters were holding back from going into the room. The firefighters were being assembled miles away, being told to wait. Fear of another attack kept them away.

There was no reason not to go into the City Room. The

rules around it being a "hot zone" should have been dropped long before. But nobody knew. Sexton claimed he still considered the room to be dangerous.

At 11.16pm another report of a second offender came in, which turned out to be bogus. This person was supposed to be near the Cathedral and therefore nowhere near the City Room.

"In your opinion – did anything go well? If so, what?" Paul Greaney asked Sexton.

"Absolutely," Sexton said.

"What went well?"

"The response by the emergency services and members of the public to the incident, I think is almost faultless."

It was an extraordinary word to use, considering his evidence, and the evidence of those who had already been to the inquiry.

Sexton carried on. "In the cold light of day, you can look at every action that people did or didn't do, but everyone tried and did their absolute best on that night, whether it was from the emergency services, members of the public, or whatever."

He told Greaney if he had to do it again, he would do exactly the same, a comment which caused a great deal of upset to the families, including Andrew and Lisa.

In the days after the attack, when debriefing his force, Sexton said at first that he did not call the other emergency services because he was overwhelmed. The inquiry heard that a training exercise a year before had already exposed problems with the FDO role being too much for one person during a major incident.

Sexton told the Kerslake Inquiry the exact same thing. He had not called fire and ambulance because he forgot in the moment. But that was not the story he gave to the Manchester Arena Inquiry. He changed his story to claim he deliberately did not contact the other emergency services in order to keep Plato a "secret".

To explain: a hot zone would mean pulling any first responders out of the City Room, even if they were helping survivors. Sexton said he did not want to tell fire or ambulance in case this happened.

So he kept it a secret, he claimed.

It was a perverse logic. Pete Weatherby questioned him about it, asking him how on earth this could be true.

"Can you help us as to why this potentially career-ending decision is not recorded at all?" Weatherby asked, taking his usual reasonable tone with the witness.

Sexton said he did not verbalise every decision he made on the night. Some of those decisions were made in his head.

Sir John Saunders stepped in. He offered him a way out.

" ... four maybe five very skilled Queen's Counsel have been trying to persuade you to say that it actually wasn't a deliberate decision not to tell the fire and ambulance, it was just a cause of complete confusion," Sir John said. " ... what they're suggesting is that it just doesn't make sense and what makes much more sense is what you have been saying at other times. 'I'm overwhelmed, I can't cope with it all, I can't deal with the fire and ambulance and with the firearms people as well.'

"So with great skill they've been trying to persuade you to say that, but you have been absolutely adamant that it was your decision. Are you going to change your mind, however many skilled people ask you the question?"

"No, sir, I came here to tell the truth," Sexton responded.

Sexton stuck to his new story to the bitter end.

The questions continued, but Andrew had heard enough. Far away in Dorset, he closed the lid of his laptop, and sat back in his chair, wondering what on earth to tell Lisa.

Enough is enough.

Chapter 27
The Power Game

Pete Weatherby was getting frustrated. And for a patient man like Weatherby, that takes a lot. The question of Saffie's survivability had become a point of serious contention between two sets of experts. In late 2020, the inquiry had asked two different sets of medical experts to get together and find any common ground they could.

Weatherby knew it would be better for Andrew and Lisa to get as much agreement as possible. If there was no agreement, then the evidence would have to be examined in great detail later in the year, so that Sir John Saunders could consider each side of the argument. Saffie's parents would have to listen to the details of their daughter's injuries be argued over in public. This was something that Weatherby was desperately trying to avoid.

On one side was the blast wave experts, made up of engineers, radiologists, and army doctors, who at first said Saffie had a chance of survival, only to change their minds.

On the other side was a second opinion provided by Dr Gareth Davies and Lt Colonel Claire Park. They both believed Saffie could have been saved.

Weatherby was trying to find some common ground, some compromise.

On 17 June, 2021, the two sets of experts met remotely

on Microsoft Teams. The meeting lasted for three hours and was chaired by Professor Anthony Bull, director of the Centre for Blast Injury Studies, who led the blast wave panel.

Davies and Park argued that the absence of medical interventions at the right time that night "made more than a minimal, negligible or trivial contribution to Saffie-Rose Roussos's death". This included limb splintage and traction, and application of tourniquets.

"We believe her injury burden was not incompatible with life," said their notes from the meeting. "Her injury pattern is consistent with the unexpected survivors who were thought to have survived in the theatres of war where early use of limb tourniquets are thought to have produced survival not previously seen."

The blast wave panel did not agree.

Weatherby knew there was no other choice. The arguments would have to be heard in full before the inquiry.

A week was set aside in December 2021. It was not ideal for the Roussos family. The meeting between the experts was in June, but the evidence would not be heard for another six months. The family was desperate for answers. It was like torture for them. They kept on pushing for an earlier date, but December was apparently the first week in which the evidence could be explored in full.

Three weeks before Christmas.

*

At the start of July, the Independent Office for Police Conduct (IOPC) announced it was investigating Dale Sexton over his evidence. It was unfortunate timing for Ian Hopkins, the former Chief Constable for Greater Manchester Police (GMP). But on 15 July, 2021, Hopkins was sworn in as a witness.

"Could you begin, please, by telling us your full name?" Paul Greaney, the counsel to the inquiry, asked.

"Ian John Hopkins."

"Mr Hopkins, on the night of the arena attack, were you the Chief Constable of Greater Manchester Police?"

"Yes, I was."

Before he started, Hopkins, tall and uniformed, said there was something he would like to say. "I wish to address this to the members of the bereaved families, those that are in court and those that are watching and listening.

"I have met many of you in person, not all of you but many, and listening to the hopes and dreams and aspirations that you had for your loved ones and how they were ripped away from you. I also saw your immense grief. All that will never leave me.

"I and my colleagues responded on 22 May with the absolute intention of doing our very best in the most challenging circumstances. In many ways, we achieved that, but I absolutely recognise that we did not always achieve our best.

"I may no longer be the Chief Constable of Greater Manchester Police, but I wish too to be associated with their apology and those condolences. Thank you."

Hopkins provided his background. In 1989 he began a career in the police in Staffordshire, moving to Northamptonshire Police in 1991. He rose to the rank of chief inspector, and was in charge of control rooms and call handling. He was a superintendent in Cheshire Police, then moved to Greater Manchester Police as an assistant Chief Constable, and later deputy chief.

His main focus as deputy was figuring out how to manage £200million in cuts due to the government's austerity measures. GMP lost 2,000 officers, along with police staff and PCSOs. "It took a huge amount out of the organisation," Hopkins told inquiry.

In October 2015, Hopkins took over as Chief Constable. He left the job in 2020.

Hopkins was not in an operational role on the night. It was not for a Chief Constable to step in and take charge, like in the TV dramas or films. In real-life, the chief has to be above operational matters, and take a wider view.

Hopkins had to deal with problems such as informing the wider public through the media, keeping Amber Rudd, the Home Secretary, updated, as well as Andy Burnham, the Mayor of Greater Manchester, who had taken office just 17 days earlier. Downing Street and Westminster had questions and looked to Hopkins for the answers. They wanted to know if Manchester was safe, and whether or not there was a wider network planning more attacks.

It was 10.57pm when Hopkins first became aware a bomb had gone off in the city centre. He was at home and about to get into bed when he was telephoned by Assistant Chief Constable Debbie Ford, the gold commander.

"There's been an explosion at the Manchester Arena, chief," she told him. "There's been fatalities. It's being treated as a terror attack. I'm the gold commander. I'm on my way to force headquarters."

"Keep me updated."

Hopkins called the leadership figures within the region to let them know the situation. He called Andy Burnham; Joanne Roney, the chief executive of Manchester City Council; Sir Richard Leese, the leader of Manchester City Council; and his own deputy, Ian Pilling.

He left his house at 11.30pm and headed to GMP headquarters, roughly a 50-mile journey. A member of his family drove so he could scan the news on his phone and take calls.

He arrived into force headquarters at just after half past midnight and went to the command suite. He didn't leave again until 10pm on the 23rd. He dealt with the Home Secretary, counter-terrorism leaders at the Met, and the media, doing those jobs so that Debbie Ford could have the space to concentrate on the operation.

But it was the former Chief Constable's evidence about the aftermath of the attack which was most of interest to the families. Andy Burnham commissioned the Kerslake Inquiry to look into the emergency services response on the night. He wanted to provide the public with some reassurance in the aftermath. It was named after Bob

Kerslake, the former head of the civil service, who wrote the report.

Kerslake travelled down to Dorset at one point to visit Andrew and Lisa, taking notes with a researcher about their experiences. It was a first chance for the public to form their opinion about how the emergency services had performed.

By now there was a number of critical stories about the night of the attack: people being evacuated on metal crash barriers, stories of survivors being left without help for hours. Kerslake was damning of the fire and rescue service; however, the police force was praised. Dale Sexton, the force duty officer, was singled out for his "dynamic" decision making on the night. The public were left with an impression that the police had been organised, practical, and made common sense decisions.

Hopkins had set up a team of lawyers and advisors to provide Kerslake with the material he needed for his report. One letter to Kerslake, which Hopkins himself signed, read: "Relevant emergency service partners were informed of the declaration of Operation Plato. Although the FDO was under considerable pressure and managing many demands, he was not overwhelmed. There was no detriment to the overall effectiveness of the operation caused by any of the above decisions/issues."

This was not correct.

The letter added: "GMP can evidence that GMFRS (the fire and rescue service), NWAS (the ambulance service), and the military were informed of the Plato declaration via specified routes within a few minutes of its declaration."

This was also not correct.

Hopkins's letter went on: "It is accepted that this was an exceptionally busy period for the FDO, but we would challenge any claim that he was overwhelmed ..."

This was definitely not correct.

Paul Greaney, the counsel to the inquiry, pointed out the problems with the letter's accuracy. "How did it come about that in a letter that was of obvious importance and which you recognised should be accurate, that something was said that was wrong?" he asked.

Hopkins said he was assured by the team he set up that the information was accurate.

"I absolutely accept it was a very grave error in that original letter to Lord Kerslake," he admitted. He said his force had corrected themselves in a follow up email a few days later. The correction, however, only went so far.

Pete Weatherby stepped up to ask his own questions on behalf of the families. "You describe the GMP response as 'outstanding', yes?" Weatherby asked.

"I think that my front-line officers and the firearms officers did an outstanding job."

"None of us would dispute that many GMP officers and others selflessly and bravely rushed to the scene and did absolutely everything they could to establish the safety of the scene and to tend to the casualties, including the dying.

However … the failures in terms of the multi-agency response was very far from outstanding, wasn't it?"

Weatherby started on Hopkins's signed letter to Kerslake – the letter which said police had contacted fire and ambulance within minutes of declaring Plato.

"Six months on (from the bomb), GMP had conducted debriefs, you'd set up a team under senior officers, a legal team, and here we are with a significant review set up by the Mayor, and a misleading picture is being painted here, isn't it? Set aside any intention, just objectively that's what's happening, isn't it?" Weatherby said.

"I think, looking at it now, some nearly four years on, I can see the point you're making. But that was clearly never anybody's intention," Hopkins said.

Hopkins blamed the force's "debrief system" not being effective, meaning information was not being passed along properly.

This was the reason why Dale Sexton could report internally that he forgot to call fire or ambulance, and the police force could claim that he had.

Weatherby went on.

"Isn't the reality here that Greater Manchester Police's orientation to Kerslake was about GMP's reputation?" Weatherby said.

"Absolutely not," said Hopkins.

"Isn't that what you were engaged in?"

"No, absolutely not …"

Hopkins and Weatherby went to and fro, Weatherby

pushing Hopkins on his letter to Kerslake, Hopkins saying he was assured the information was correct.

Weatherby may be the voice of reason when it comes to his courtroom presence, but like any good barrister, he likes to finish with a hard-hitting question.

"Just finally this, Mr Hopkins," Weatherby said. "At GMP were you and your senior leadership team acting with candour here … or were you focused on defending Greater Manchester Police's reputation?"

It was a stunning question to have to ask of a former Chief Constable for one of the UK's largest police forces.

"You asked me that question this morning and my answer remains the same: absolutely not," Hopkins said.

Hopkins was not deliberately trying to deceive Lord Kerslake, the inquiry would later determine, and was simply relaying the information that he had been told. Information which was completely inaccurate.

Chapter 28

Runaways

By the autumn of 2021, Andrew and Lisa were ready to move out of their rented house and into their new bungalow. It was a big step for the family. They hoped their new home would help them put down roots in Dorset, and create a safe space for their new lives. The village gave them a feeling of anonymity and privacy, and easy access to the local beach.

Lisa no longer needed her wheelchair. She had made good progress, but she would never feel absolutely comfortable walking around on her own, feeling like she might lose her balance at any moment.

For that reason, she rarely left the house without Andrew, who would usually be holding her hand if they were walking in the street, perhaps on a day trip to Dorchester or Poole. In Poole they might buy a coffee and sit on the front and watch the people go by, enjoying the sight of day-trippers having fun on the beach.

Andrew had redesigned the interior. He had created a house with wide open spaces, which Lisa managed to quickly fill with collectibles and trinkets. He had created an open-plan kitchen with a log burner in the corner of the room. Wood for the burner was expensive, and Lisa would enjoy spotting logs and branches on the roadside for

Andrew to stick in the boot. "Come on, you can pick that up!"

Saffie's bedroom was set up, of course. Her room was decorated with her framed cartoon drawings. One of those drawings shows the whole family in a row in doodle-form. Lisa is wearing a yellow polka-dot dress; Andrew has a black triangle for a goatee; Xander is next with a big smile on his face; then there was Saffie herself, holding Binky on a lead.

On her bedpost hangs a little straw hat, which she often wore on holidays with the family. Her favourite denim jacket is on a hook, almost as if she had just hung it up there. A pair of her sunglasses sits on a shelf, along with various birthday cards.

Andrew and Lisa are constantly in her room. They use her wardrobe space and her cupboards for their own clothes. They are constantly inside it. That's the way they wanted it. They didn't want her room to become some dusty place, shut away.

They use the room as a guest bedroom. People who stay in the room will sometimes leave behind a present for Saffie. Sam once stayed and left behind a cactus, with her name on the pot. Another time Janine stayed and left behind an ornament of a bee.

They were extremely happy with the house. Xander settled in quickly. Binky enjoyed running in and out of the garden, barking ferociously at anybody who dared to knock on the door. They filled the flower beds with Saffie-Rose shrubs.

Lisa would look forward to her visits from Ashlee, who became pregnant. Part of Lisa had hoped the baby might be a boy. She was scared that a girl might remind her too much of Saffie, and what she had lost. But as soon as Ever-Rose was born, Lisa's fears were lifted, and she immediately fell in love. Ever-Rose became a regular visitor to her grandmother, who knew time was precious. She was determined to spend as much of it as possible with her granddaughter, whom she loved unconditionally.

Andrew and Lisa waited patiently for Saffie's week of evidence, but it was like mental torture. In the background, more evidence was emerging of suspects connected to the attack.

Many of the families were convinced that Salman Abedi and his brother, Hashem, did not act alone. Simon Barraclough, the detective in charge of the criminal investigation, has often said the evidence "remains under constant review".

Ismail Abedi, the eldest brother of Salman and Hashem, had been living in a semi-detached house in an upmarket part of south Manchester, calling himself "Ben Romdhan", sculpted beard, chest puffed out from his sessions in the gym.

He was arrested under the Terrorism Act the morning after the arena bombing, but released under investigation. His DNA was discovered in a car used to store the explosives. In 2015, he had been stopped at the border and police found extremist material on his phone. The inquiry wanted to hear his evidence.

He would know plenty of information about his brothers which might help understand why they had carried out the attack, or how they had been radicalised. He denied knowing anything about what his brothers were planning.

He agreed to give evidence to the inquiry on one condition: he would be provided with immunity from criminal prosecution no matter what evidence he gave to the hearings. *If he has nothing to hide, why ask for immunity?* Andrew thought.

In June 2021, Sir John Saunders, the inquiry chairman, turned down Ismail's immunity application, saying it would be an "affront to justice". He served Ismail with a legal notice requiring him to attend in person to give evidence on 21 October.

On 28 August, he turned up at Manchester Airport, and attempted to leave the country. The police stopped him. He turned up the very next day with tickets for a new flight to Istanbul. This time he was allowed to leave. Police said they had no legal power to prevent him from leaving the country.

Ismail never returned. He was convicted in his absence in July 2022 of failing to appear at the inquiry and an arrest warrant has been issued. At the time of writing he has not yet been found.

Likewise, other suspects were allowed to leave the UK, never to return, such as Elyas Elmehdi, a drug dealer, who allowed Abedi to park his car outside his apartment in south Manchester as a favour. The car boot contained the bomb parts and explosive chemicals.

Elmehdi was seen checking on the car, and his friends were also seen checking on the car, in the lead-up to the attack. He was never charged with any terror offence. He left the country, and at the time of writing has not been found.

A third individual, who helped purchase chemicals for the bomb, also left the country to live in Libya. He claims he knew nothing about why Hashem Abedi wanted such a large quantity of sulphuric acid. He denies any involvement and has never been charged with terrorism offences. He has since returned to the UK to live.

Chapter 29
The Truth about Saffie

Monday, 29 November, 2021.
The week had finally arrived. For the next five days, Saffie's evidence would be heard. Eleven different medical experts would give their opinions, and the inquiry would also hear from those who were inside the City Room with Saffie. This was an important moment for the inquiry and Sir John Saunders, who had to maintain the confidence of the families, otherwise his inquiry would become flawed.

Saffie was one of the most high-profile victims of the attack, for a number of reasons. She was the youngest, she was extremely photogenic, and her family were decent, hard-working people. The Roussos family were a family who the nation could look at and recognise as being like their own.

If it could happen to them, it could happen to anyone, people would think, after reading about their experiences.

That morning, Andrew and Lisa walked into Manchester Magistrates' Court holding hands. They sat in the families' room, close to the room where the hearings took place, sitting with their legal team, discussing what was about to happen over black coffee.

Pete Weatherby knew it was going to be a tough week. They were about to hear the sort of detail about their child's injuries which no parent would ever want to know. They would need every bit of strength to get through the next five days. Christmas was looming. Once a time of joy for the Roussos family, these days it was more difficult.

Andrew was worried the week might send Lisa into a spiral of depression after she'd fought so hard to get herself into a good place, doing her exercises, going swimming, walking on the beach. He prayed this would not set her back.

That Monday, Sophie Cartwright QC, dressed in a dark suit, was acting as the barrister to the inquiry. Her manner was serious, but also had warmth, as she presented the order of running to Sir John Saunders, standing at her desk as she addressed the room.

Sir John made a point of thanking Weatherby and his team for the extent of their cooperation. "I know Mr Roussos will have had an input into that and obviously, as we go along, if there are things that the families are concerned about, then of course we will do our best to meet with any concerns that they do have."

He then got to the crux of the matter. There was a difference of opinion with the experts. It was not going to be easy evidence to hear, for the parents or for the inquiry. "I'm sorry that there has been that difference of opinion, but these things do happen, and I will have to determine it to the best of my ability," he said.

It would be down to Sir John to decide whether Saffie had a chance of surviving or not.

Cartwright took a moment to sketch out Saffie's character and personality, using Lisa's own words. "Saffie was a sensitive soul who loved and gave generously," Cartwright said. "She would talk to people and have their complete attention, all the time being her gentle, funny self."

Her school now had a heritage plaque dedicated to her, Cartwright said. Her teachers had been asked for three words to describe Saffie. They had used "beautiful", "captivating", and "kind".

On the 174th day of sitting, the inquiry finally arrived at the evidence of how Saffie died on 22 May, 2017.

Some readers might find the following section particularly distressing.

*

The inquiry used CCTV, body-camera footage, witness evidence and medical records to provide an account of what happened to Saffie after the bomb was detonated.

Minutes after the explosion, Saffie was seen holding herself up for a few seconds before lying back down. She was lying on her back, and was seen raising up her left arm.

At 10.35pm, Paul Reid, a poster seller, saw her injured and came to her side. He asked what her name was. He thought she said her name was Sophie. Saffie told him she was eight years old and asked for her mother.

Reid could see that Saffie's legs were badly injured.

"Saffie asked him what had happened," Cartwright told

the inquiry, her voice steady but her tone carrying the weight of the words. "He knew her injuries were serious, so he stayed with her. Saffie put her hand up to move her hair out of her eyes. Paul put her hand down and told her not to worry, before moving her hair out of her eyes for her."

At 10.37pm, Reid and Saffie were joined by the arena merchandise manager. "Stay with me, baby," Reid told Saffie.

"Everything is going to be ok," the manager said. "Help is on its way."

Saffie was drifting in and out of consciousness. The merchandise manager left to look for her staff, not knowing who had survived the blast and who had not.

At 10.40pm, Reid was seen on the CCTV cameras putting up his hand to catch the attention of the arena medics, who were dressed in green uniforms, carrying first aid bags.

One of the arena medics, employed by first aid providers Emergency Training UK (ETUK), approached Saffie. She cut her leggings open to expose her right hip and thigh to check for bleeding.

The medic had a communication radio with an earpiece in her right ear. "We're stopping catastrophic bleeding only. If they're not breathing, leave them," said somebody in her control room.

A man was handing out bottles of water. Reid asked Saffie if she wanted a drink. She said yes, so he gave her a couple of mouthfuls.

She said she wanted more, but he said no, as he thought she might need an operation.

Saffie started shaking. Reid asked her if she was cold and when she said yes he took off his coat and put it over her. She was struggling to breathe, but tried to talk to him.

Reid told her not to bother trying to talk but to concentrate on breathing. Saffie was losing consciousness. Reid shouted at her to wake up. This happened several times. He would shout what he thought was her name – "SOPHIE, SOPHIE" – until she opened her eyes.

At 10.41pm, another ETUK medic joined Reid and the first medic. She remained for a short time before leaving and returning again slightly later. A third ETUK medic approached Saffie and stayed for thirty seconds before leaving.

Sergeant Dale Edwards, from British Transport Police (BTP), approached. "Stay awake," he told Saffie. "Keep your eyes open."

Edwards told Reid to keep talking to her, to keep her awake until the paramedics came. He decided to go to other casualties since Saffie was conscious and breathing and had somebody with her.

Edwards told the inquiry he thought the paramedics would arrive soon to give Saffie the help she needed. This never happened.

By now it was getting close to half an hour since the bomb exploded and no paramedic had arrived to help Saffie. Their sirens could be heard outside. But nobody was coming in.

Saffie was turning pale and grey. Her condition was

deteriorating. Reid shouted for help. An ETUK first aider came and turned Saffie on her side and saw a wound to her lower back. She applied a bandage to it and told Reid to apply pressure and keep her talking.

At 10.51pm, Sergeant Peter Wilcock, from BTP, directed off-duty nurse Bethany Crook to Saffie.

Wilcock thought Saffie was dead, she was so grey. He shook her on the shoulder. Saffie's eyes moved. "An ambulance is on the way," he told her.

Wilcock tried to look at her injuries. In the chaos and with no equipment, it felt impossible, he said.

At 10.53pm, Bethany Crook was seen on the floor tending to Saffie. Crook was a registered nurse. She was at the concert with her daughter when the bomb went off.

Crook told the inquiry that she remembered Saffie being on her back at this point. Reid was with her and positioned on her upper left side, loosely cradling her. Reid was shouting at her to stay awake.

Saffie was quite still, according to those who remained at her side.

Crook held her hand. Her breathing was rapid, her diaphragm distended and her pulse was high. Crook thought she had internal injuries. She didn't want to move her, and thought it was best to wait for professional assistance and medical supplies to arrive.

At 10.54pm, advanced paramedic Patrick Ennis was seen leaning over Saffie, who was still with Reid and Crook. He is seen moving to another part of the City Room.

Ennis was the first paramedic in the room and was there, as was the policy, to conduct a "sweep" and report back to his commanders about the condition of all the casualties. He would come in the room later to carry out triage. By that time, Saffie had been taken out.

At 10.55pm, Reid grabbed a large advertising board and placed it on the floor near to where Saffie was lying. With the help of a police officer he moved Saffie onto the advertising board.

"There you go, gorgeous," Crook said.

"Let's lift her up and get her out of here," said a police officer.

Crook was applying pressure to a pad on Saffie's right leg. "It's alright my darling," Crook told her. "It's alright."

Her eyes were open, and she was holding her stomach. The situation felt desperate. Just desperate.

"We've got to get her out of here," Reid shouted.

At 10.56pm, the group were making their way through the wreckage of the room, carrying Saffie on the advertising board. The group was made up of three police officers, two members of the public including Reid, and Crook. She was slipping around on the board. It was not fit for purpose.

Saffie's eyes were closing.

"This way, this way, this way," shouted PC McLaughlin, one of the officers helping to carry her. He moved as if to head towards the Victoria Station exit.

"Which way are we going?" Reid shouted.

"Ok, we'll go this way, then" McLaughlin replied.

They headed towards the Trinity Way exit with Reid walking backwards.

"There's no ambulances at the back," somebody shouted, meaning the back of the arena.

"Stay with us, stay with us, sweetheart," Crook said.

They took her down the stairs heading towards the Trinity Way link tunnel. They were struggling badly with the makeshift stretcher. It was awkward and heavy.

"Careful, careful, careful, one step at a time," shouted PC McLaughlin.

Crook checked her pulse. "Right, you stay with me, my darling, you squeeze my hand, don't you go on me, darling."

She took hold of Saffie's right hand. The group continued to carry Saffie down the steps.

"Come on, baby, come on, princess," Reid shouted, saying the same thing on repeat. "Come on, princess."

The group sped up as they headed along the low-ceiling tunnel towards Trinity Way. Crook kept checking to see if she was breathing.

At 10.58pm, they emerged from the tunnel. They put the advertising board onto the pavement.

PC McLaughlin ran down Trinity Way towards police vehicles in the distance. He called on his radio.

"2608, got a critical – 2608, got a critically injured girl, Trinity Way, outside," he said breathlessly. "Need an ambulance here, now."

"1711 can your paramedic go to that, please?" replied the operator.

An unmarked police car pulled up.

It was half an hour since the bomb exploded and there were no ambulances at the back of the arena, where many had gathered.

The group considered trying to put Saffie and the advertising board into the back of the unmarked police car. But the board was just too big.

"We need an ambulance," Crook says, feeling her pulse, which was weak.

By 11pm, Saffie was not moving or making any sounds. Her eyes were barely open.

Crook held her head and tilted it back to keep her airway open. "That's it, gorgeous girl, that's it, you stay, you stay."

At just after 11pm an ambulance arrived with a female paramedic and a female ambulance technician.

"A33, yes, affirmative," said the ambulance crew to their control operator. "We've just been flagged over by the police. We've got an eight-year-old that we are going to deal with."

The ambulance was on scene for 16 minutes before it left for the hospital. Crook briefed the paramedics on what she knew. "Pulse, spinal injuries, she's got back injuries, leg lacerations ... We're trying to secure her airway and she's in and out of consciousness."

Saffie was moved from the advertising board onto a proper stretcher which had been taken from the back of the ambulance.

At 11.06pm Saffie was lying on her back on the

ambulance trolley. She was not moving and hardy making a sound.

One of the ambulance crew placed an oxygen mask over Saffie. "There you go sweetheart, there you go." They secured Saffie to the trolley. At 11.15pm the ambulance started off to hospital.

The paramedic thought Saffie could go into cardiac arrest at any moment. She needed to be in hospital. The paramedic attached monitoring equipment. Heart rate, blood pressure, respiratory rate and oxygen levels.

Saffie then asked a question. "Am I going to die?"

The female paramedic reassured her and tried to comfort her as best she could. She looked waxy and had blue lips.

By this point she had lost a lot of blood. She was pulling at her oxygen mask and it appeared to be causing her distress. The paramedic knew she was losing blood from her legs, probably due to internal bleeding and shrapnel wounds.

She said she considered using a combat tourniquet but thought because her legs were swollen she would not be able to apply it high enough for it to be effective.

The ambulance crew radioed ahead to Manchester Children's Hospital. By the time they arrived at 11.26pm she was quiet and no longer making any noise. It was 52 minutes since the bomb.

The ambulance crew was shown into the resuscitation area where a team of doctors was prepared and waiting.

Saffie was the first casualty they received from the arena.

The paramedic said her name was "Steph". They gave doctors an update. "She's been involved in the incident at the MEN where we believe a nail bomb has gone off. Her airway is clear. She has bilateral air entry, but as you can see, she has massive blood loss due to the multiple injuries to her legs. I am sorry, I couldn't get a line in to give her fluids or tranexamic acid."

The nurses and doctors took over. Saffie was hooked up to a heart monitor. But her heartrate was dropping.

Dr Rachel Jenner was a consultant in the paediatric emergency department at the hospital. Jenner was in charge of the trauma team which cared for Saffie. It was clear straight away she had suffered terrible injuries. Saffie was making weak, gasping breaths which then stopped. They started chest compressions and intubating Saffie.

She was given adrenaline and emergency blood transfusions. The resuscitation attempts by Jenner and the other doctors, surgeons and nurses were unsuccessful. The cardiac monitor was showing no electrical activity of the heart. She was not breathing and had no pulse.

Four cycles of cardiac compressions were completed before the team decided to stop. They considered a last-ditch surgical procedure called a thoracotomy which would have meant opening up her chest to search for internal damage.

The doctors decided against it. She was too far gone, they thought. She could not be brought back. Her time of death was given by the doctors as 11.40pm. Saffie's fight was over.

The inquiry took a break for lunch, then returned at 2.10pm.

"Sir, the gentleman in the witness box is Andrew Roussos," Cartwright told Sir John Saunders, "but can I also indicate that present in the hearing room now is Saffie's mum, Lisa Roussos, who is supported by her friend."

Andrew, wearing a grey suit and dark red tie, his goatee beard neat and trimmed, was sworn in.

Never one to hold back, Andrew decided it was time to have the family's voice heard. Like his previous speech, it was not part of the inquiry's plan for the day.

"Sir, may I just say a couple of words as Saffie's father? After that summary, I just feel the need to just express what we've just heard. I've just got a couple of words now to say, if I may.

"I would like to say that I see myself as an uneducated, clever man, but in a roomful of educated people I have never heard so many excuses, so much justification that the response on 22 May was somehow acceptable.

"As a human being, a father, I cannot live with myself if I don't voice this. The response on that night was shameful and inadequate. Everybody in the City Room was let down and the people that excuse it should feel shame. What Saffie went through, I'll never forgive. That poor little girl hung in there for someone to come and help her. What she received was a bloody advertisement board and untrained people doing the best they could.

"Even when she got into the door of the professional ambulance that got involved, they didn't do much more. I'll come back to it, again, sir. Lessons learned? What can we learn from this?

"As Saffie's dad, I wish I had known more about how bad things are, so I could have protected her, and I apologise for speaking my mind or if I offend anybody, but what I'm saying is not directed to any individual. Sir, we are human beings in a modern world and the response of the security services on this atrocity should go down in history as one of the worst failures from start to finish and that's what we should learn from this.

"Thank you."

The room stayed silent. It felt like Andrew's anger could be felt in every part of it.

And who was to say he should feel otherwise? Who among them could tell him that he was wrong to feel that way?

Cartwright asked Andrew to describe what happened that evening, searching across Manchester for his family, only to find Lisa in hospital fighting for her life. He described hearing the news about Saffie's death from Russ, the detective.

Andrew finished. Sir John Saunders took a moment before he spoke. "It's an unbelievable nightmare," he said, shaking his head, "and living through that must have been absolutely awful."

"Sir, my thing is that – reliving it, I've got no choice and I feel it's a need and a responsibility to do my best to make sure this doesn't happen to another family. I feel it's something I owe to the world."

Sir John nodded. "It's just a surreal place to find yourself. I share your wishes ... I haven't had to live through what you've lived through to drive you, but it has been inspirational to hear from you."

Lisa was next.

It was her first-time giving evidence in person. She had previously appeared at the inquiry in a video during Saffie's pen portrait. This time she wanted her voice to be heard from the witness box.

It was not an easy experience for Lisa. Andrew was outgoing, but Lisa's nature was to be private. She found it hard being in the media spotlight, and she was conscious the media would be watching, as she stepped into the witness box, dressed in a smart navy jacket and white top.

She didn't want people to see her cry. She didn't want people to remember her like that.

She wanted to make Saffie proud.

Cartwright started. "You tell us in your witness statement what we've already heard about Saffie today, that she was a big fan of Ariana Grande?"

"She was, yes," Lisa said, her voice gentle but firm.

"She watched her on all the American kids' TV shows?"

"Yes, she did."

"And you only knew of her through Saffie?"

"Yes."

"Were you a fan too?" Sir John asked, a well-meaning but slightly awkward attempt to lighten the mood.

Lisa smiled and shook her head. "Er, no."

It had been Andrew's idea to buy the Ariana Grande tickets, she said. She had been apprehensive because it would be busy at the concert. "I was a bit worried, I didn't really want her to go, but then when Ariana Grande came and Saffie knew she was only in Manchester and we could have taken her, I knew she'd be disappointed, so we went ahead and bought the tickets."

She told the inquiry about Christmas day. Xander getting his drum kit, Saffie the tickets to the concert.

Cartwright asked her about the night itself. Lisa described being dropped off by Craig, going through a minimum of security checks to enter the building, finding their seats. Then the concert starting, Saffie so happy, dancing and singing.

She arrived at the moment where the concert ended, and everybody was leaving.

"Because we were at the back, it was just a few steps up and it was the exit," she said. "We all started walking out and I can remember Ashlee being ahead of us.

"Saffie had my left hand and my arm was outstretched, she was, like, pulling me because she wanted to go and see her dad and Xander. Then, the next minute … Sorry."

She paused, gathering up the courage to speak about the worst moment of her life, when Saffie got hurt.

"Have a glass of water if you like. I'm told it sometimes helps," Sir John said.

Lisa sipped the glass of water in front of her.

Cartwright continued. "It's right, isn't it, that the memory of Saffie pulling your arms and being outstretched was the last thing you remember before the explosion?"

"Yes."

Lisa told the inquiry her memories of being in the room after the bomb. Lying there. Trying to move her arms and her legs but nothing moving. Forcing herself to stay awake. How it felt like hours before anybody approached her. And when somebody did, managing to say a single word: "Saffie."

Cartwright described Lisa's injuries. How when she arrived at hospital there was only a small chance she would live.

Sir John Saunders asked about Ashlee, and noted that Lisa now had a grandchild.

"I do, yes."

She had almost come to the end of her evidence. Now was the moment she had been preparing for. She cleared her throat, and looked up to Sir John. "Can I say something?" she said.

"Yes," Sir John said, knowing there was no way he could refuse, whatever she was about to say.

The room was full of pre-eminent medical experts; professors of engineering and medical science; renowned barristers; leading solicitors and journalists; and a retired high court judge who had presided over some of the most high-profile cases in the land.

But not a single one of them had more of a right to speak in that room than Lisa.

"I want to thank those who tried to help Saffie that night and for being with her," she said. "I also want to say to the professionals, like the emergency services and MI5, that this inquiry isn't about protecting your job, your reputation or your uniform.

"We understand the sheer panic and fear you were faced with that night, but until you admit the failings, how can there be a positive change?"

The people in that room thought about those words. Sir John, included. They seemed to mean more, coming from Lisa.

"Thank you," Sir John said at last. "And thank you particularly for thanking those who tried to help on the night. I am sure that will mean a great deal to them."

Sir John decided to say a few words himself. "I just want to say something. I know that both of you (Andrew and Lisa) may be going after this and I well understand that. Just let me say something about Saffie if you don't mind.

"Saffie won the hearts of all who met her. She brought happiness to many people with her wonderfully open smile and ability to make people laugh. We have talked a lot in this inquiry of the loss of potential and that is certainly true of Saffie, but she had clearly achieved a great deal at the time she died.

"She could, so her father says, like any eight-year-old, be naughty, but somehow she always managed to win people over, whatever she had done. She was a beautiful, talented girl.

"Her family have gone through the most appalling experiences and lost someone who was very precious to them. What a waste of a very special person. She was an innocent child who had done nothing to deserve what happened to her.

"Whatever the reason for this appalling attack, it had nothing whatsoever to do with Saffie. Thank you."

*

After giving evidence, Andrew and Lisa were shown by Pete Weatherby and Nicola Brook into a small side room used in the court building for families to debrief with their legal teams. Brook was standing at the door, about to walk inside, when she looked down the corridor.

Paul Reid, the poster seller and forklift truck driver, was standing in the corridor with a woman, waiting to give evidence.

"Paul Reid is standing outside," Brook said. "Do you want me to introduce you?"

Andrew and Lisa looked at one another. They both immediately stood up. "I want to meet him," Lisa said.

They had wanted to meet him for years. Both of them knew they might never have the opportunity again.

Reid had given an interview to the BBC saying he was still haunted by what had happened that night. He had described it as, being "like yesterday. I can still smell the smoke in that foyer. Still hear the alarms when I go to sleep, when I close my eyes. I'm first aid trained, but the most I'd done is put a plaster on. To step in that foyer, it was carnage. It was a war zone."

But he had done something which meant more to Andrew and Lisa than words can ever express. He had stayed with Saffie. When others panicked and ran away, he had stayed.

He was a hero. They approached Reid and he saw them. Reid started to get upset. He knew who they were. The woman with Reid encouraged him to go and speak to them. "Go on. You might never get the chance again," she said.

Reid could hardly look at them. Lisa stepped forward and hugged him. "I just want to say – thank you, Paul. Thank you for being with Saffie," she said, crying.

Andrew shook Paul's hand. He had wished so many times that he had gone into the City Room to find Saffie. When he was outside the arena searching for her, all that had stopped him from going in was a police officer telling him everyone had already been evacuated. Andrew would have done anything to be at Saffie's side in those final moments.

But he also knew Saffie had not been alone, thanks to Paul. "Thank you, Paul," Andrew said. "You stayed with her. And that means the world to us."

Reid could barely speak. "I've got to go," he said, quietly.

He walked down the corridor and into the inquiry room, where he would give his own evidence about what happened that night.

Andrew and Lisa watched him go. Whether he knew it or not, he would always be a hero to them.

Chapter 30
Davies and Park

The evidence laying out the facts of Saffie's case had been heard. Thursday, 2 December was set aside to hear the opinions of the blast wave panel of experts who would interpret that evidence and give their opinion of Saffie's chances of survival.

Likewise, Friday would then hear the second opinion from two of the UK's leading emergency response practitioners who did not accept the view of the blast wave panel. Sir John Saunders, as the chairman, would listen to that evidence, then come to his conclusions in his final report. First, though, it was the turn of the blast wave panel.

"Sir, good morning," Paul Greaney told the chairman. "Today we are going to hear from the blast wave panel, each member of which is in the hearing room."

All five experts had arrived that Thursday to be on hand to provide their arguments and opinions. There was Professor Bull, head of bioengineering at Imperial College London, where he led the Centre for Blast Injury Studies; Lieutenant Colonel Dr Mark Ballard, from the Royal Army Medical Corps, who was a radiologist; Colonel Professor Jonathan Clasper, a serving officer with the British Royal Army Medical Corps until 2019, and a consultant in orthopaedic surgery until 2021; Alan Hepper, an engineer at the Defence Science and Technology Laboratory, where he carried out research to understand the effect of injuries from military weapons; and Colonel Professor Peter Mahoney, a consultant in anaesthesia, who joined the Territorial Army in 1980 and had previously deployed to Iraq and Afghanistan where he had treated people with blast injuries.

Professor Bull was the leader of the panel. He explained how the panel had worked. He said they had come to a "collective view" on their findings, rather than providing five individual opinions and that their work had been to look at how the 22 people who died in the arena bomb had come to die.

" ... the question we were answering was survivability, to be specific," Professor Bull said. "And in all of this, we erred on the side of survivability unless we had strong evidence and clear evidence that the injuries were unsurvivable."

To help them they had examined the radiology, the video footage, and the witness statements for each case. They had looked at what interventions might have been taken to help the individual survive, and whether that might have saved them.

"A phrase has been used: wargaming," Professor Bull said. "And that was conducted for each one of the fatalities where appropriate."

"So essentially working out whether the outcome may have been different if there had been different interventions," Paul Greaney, counsel to the inquiry, asked.

"That's correct."

Andrew and Lisa had asked for the second opinion after learning that the blast wave panel had changed its mind about Saffie. In their first report they said she was unlikely to survive, meaning she had a chance, no matter how slim. They later amended their findings to say she had "nil" chance.

Greaney turned to the first report from the blast wave experts. "Saffie-Rose Roussos sustained multiple secondary blast injuries with two of particular significance and an overall high burden of injury," Greaney read. "Her injuries were unlikely to be survivable with current advanced medical treatment."

"That's correct," Professor Bull said. " ... meaning that survival would not be expected."

"But it was not being excluded."

"That's correct."

"Was not impossible, in other words. In due course, you produced a second report," Greaney said.

The second report said that her lung injury would have caused significant shortage of oxygen to her organs. The leg injuries were also associated with severe bleeding.

"'The injuries were not amenable to treatment outside hospital,'" Greaney said, reading from their second report. "'Based on the video footage, witness statements and the above information, we believe Saffie-Rose Roussos' injuries were unsurvivable with current advanced medical treatment, even if speedier admission to hospital had taken place.'"

Greaney considered for a moment what he had just read. "So, you will agree that there had been a change in your opinion as a panel between the first report and the second report?"

"That is a clarification based on our approach that erred on the side of survivability until we had further evidence, yes," Professor Bull said.

Quite an important "clarification", since it meant the difference between life or death.

Greaney pushed on. "I think you're agreeing that there had been a change that she had moved from being unlikely to survive to being unsurvivable, which means no possibility of survival."

"That's correct."

Greaney asked how their opinion had come to change. Professor Bull said the additional evidence which had changed their minds between the two reports was viewing the police body-worn camera footage, which they had not previously seen. "That confirmed in and of itself that this was unsurvivable," he said.

Professor Bull argued that the footage showed she had severe difficulties in breathing which they thought were related to a lung injury – in this case blast lung – which, combined with the leg injuries, would have been fatal. He also said they had viewed more medical scans and further witness statements since the first report.

"In your second report you express the view that I've set out that Saffie was unsurvivable," Greaney said. "Does it remain the opinion of the panel that Saffie was unsurvivable?"

"Yes, it does."

The panel's view had not changed.

Saffie had been able to survive for more than an hour. She had sat up and taken sips of water. She was able to ask for her mother. She was even able to ask in the ambulance about whether she might die.

Even so, the five experts had decided she had nil chance of survival following the blast.

"So may I ask you," Greaney said, "how is it possible to exclude the possibility, even if a remote possibility, that Saffie would have survived if given different or additional or earlier treatment?"

"There is no evidence anywhere from the personal experience of the panel members, from any of the scientific literature, from any of the data that we will present ... that anyone has previously survived such a constellation of injuries, even with the most appropriate medical care ..." Professor Bull said.

Andrew and Lisa were unconvinced.

Why had they formed an opinion about Saffie in the first place without seeing all the evidence?

To them, this made no sense.

It had shaken their confidence in their methods. They had turned to Pete Weatherby to find a second opinion, which the inquiry had permitted.

Weatherby would later praise Sir John Saunders for this

decision, describing him as "fair minded" throughout the process, and somebody who had made a genuine attempt to help the families uncover as much of the truth about what happened as was possible.

Andrew and Lisa had sat and heard the evidence of the blast wave panel. Tomorrow it would be the turn of Davies and Park. And their findings could not have been more different.

*

On Friday, Dr Gareth Davies and Lieutenant Colonel Claire Park were sworn in as witnesses. As was usual, the hearing was provided with their background and experience before being asked about their evidence. Dr Davies was a consultant in emergency medicine and pre-hospital care with more than 25 years of experience doing each.

From 1996 to 2019, he was the medical director for London's Air Ambulance, with responsibility for the care and treatment strategies of over 40,000 seriously injured patients. During this time, he had attended and provided medical treatment at numerous major incidents.

This included the IRA's Bishopsgate bombing in 1993; the Canary Wharf bombing in 1996; the Aldwych bus bomb in 1996; the Southall rail disaster in 1997; the Paddington rail disaster in 1999; and the Potters Bar rail disaster in 2002.

"You were also involved in providing medical treatment in the aftermath of the 7/7 bombings?" Greaney said.

"Yes. And there were several other minor bombing incidents in London, such as the Soho attack, which we also attended," Davies said.

Dr Davies had contributed to national working groups on trauma and major incidents, and had developed a technique to stop patients bleeding to death from pelvic injuries outside of hospital using a procedure which sees a balloon inserted at the top of the thigh. The technique was now common practice in London.

He has been published in more than 60 peer-reviewed papers, and lectured in pre-hospital care at Queen Mary University of London. Simply put, he was one of the most experienced practitioners of emergency medicine in the UK.

Next to him was Lieutenant Colonel Dr Claire Park, who Davies had teamed up with to write their second-opinion report. Park's CV was also impressive. A consultant in pre-hospital care, critical care and anaesthesia for the British Army, she had been deployed to Afghanistan three times as a member of the Medical Emergency Response Team (MERT) and to North Africa with a small forward surgical team.

She had experience treating patients who had been severely injured by improvised explosive devices, similar to the one let off by Abedi.

She was the clinical governance lead for MERT between 2013 and 2016, and has held NHS consultant roles. She was also a major incident lead with London's air ambulance. In that role, she was the post-incident lead for the Fishmongers' Hall and London Bridge attacks.

"Through those various roles and responsibilities, do you commonly see patients within minutes of serious injury being sustained?" asked Greaney.

"Yes, through the air ambulance work on a weekly basis," Park answered.

"And do you therefore see patients who are literally bleeding to death?" Greaney said.

"Sadly, we do, on a repeated basis."

Greaney took a moment to assess their expertise. "I'm sure I can be excused saying that, plainly, you each have very considerable experience in pre-hospital care and emergency medicine," Greaney said. "That will be beyond doubt, but as you'll appreciate it's important to see whether there are any limits on the expertise that the two of you have. May I ask both of you, Dr Davies first of all, do you have expertise such as to enable you to comment on the question of whether, had Saffie reached hospital in a better condition, she would have survived surgery?"

"Yes, I do," Dr Davies said.

"Do you have that personally or is it experience that the two of you have in combination?"

"Personally," Dr Davies answered.

"And Dr Park?"

"Yes, I look after casualties within a hospital, both in the UK and have done abroad, deployed in the military."

Greaney moved to their evidence in relation to Saffie. "

... you attach importance to the fact that Saffie was able to survive until hospital, a period of over 50 minutes, without any substantial medical invention?" Greaney said.

"Yes, that's correct," Davies said.

Davies and Park believed the period she managed to survive meant the vascular damage, or bleeding, cannot have been as serious, and the lung damage cannot have been as serious, as the blast wave panel had made out. They also thought that if the injuries to Saffie were as serious as the panel had said then she would have died within minutes.

But she did not.

Dr Park said it was the time Saffie managed to survive with a bare minimum of medical intervention which stood out. She was hurt by the bomb at 10.31pm and arrived at the hospital at 11.24pm. "It's basically an hour, and I think we see people who are going to die often die before that time," Park said.

They both thought Saffie's injuries could have been helped with some basic medical interventions which would have hugely improved her chances of survival.

Davies said that there were first aiders in the City Room with the necessary skills and equipment to provide Saffie with three interventions which would have probably saved her life: splintage, traction and tourniquets. This would have helped stop the bleeding from Saffie's legs and it was her loss of blood which led to her cardiac arrest.

"Are those the three interventions that you consider

ought to have been applied in the City Room?" Greaney asked.

"Yes," Davies replied.

Splintage would have meant bringing Saffie's legs out to length, which would have reduced the bleeding by bringing the muscles down to their normal position, in tight application around the fracture site.

A traction splint could have been used, which is a medical device which uses straps, a metal rod and a mechanical device to apply traction to the limb. Splints can help align and stabilise fractures, which can reduce pain and bleeding. A simple box splint could also have been used in the room that day – basically a piece of padded plastic with straps.

Davies and Park used splints on a daily basis and they said it will transform a patient and their prospects.

"You can see it with your own eyes, the impact those manoeuvres have on the patient," Davies said. "A patient will be pale, like Saffie was, and in pain. Bringing the leg out to length can bring back her colour, bring down the heart rate, it reduces the bleeding."

The next thing that would have helped Saffie was traction. This would have meant pulling Saffie's thigh out to its normal length, so the bones pull into their normal position and the muscles become tightly applied around the fracture.

"How you do that is very simple, very simple," Dr Davies said. "You simply put your hand around the knee, you put your hand around the foot, and you pull. Sometimes in adults, you will get a lot of spasm in the muscles and you have to pull quite strongly. In children it's usually very easy and you simply pull the leg out to length." He said the technique would take a minute or two for both legs.

North West Ambulance Service had previously suggested to the inquiry they do not splint in that situation or do the manoeuvres Davies was suggesting.

"It is standard practice," Dr Davies said. "We see it happening in London."

Dr Davies said the third technique that would have helped Saffie was to apply a tourniquet on her legs. "Saffie was bleeding to death in her legs," he said. " ... at that point, the application of a tourniquet, I think, would be more than reasonable."

A tourniquet could have been put at the top of her legs to stop the bleeding. Some of the eyewitnesses said they did not see much blood and so did not think Saffie required a tourniquet.

This was a common misconception, Davies said. Bleeding can be happening internally as well as externally, so a person should look not just for blood, but also a swelling of the leg, in deciding whether to use a tourniquet or not. A tourniquet will help with both internal and external bleeding, Davies pointed out.

"I would always err on the side of caution and put a high tourniquet on," he said.

"So let's assume that in the City Room each of those measures had been taken. What is your view about the impact of those measures on Saffie's survivability?" Greaney said.

" … the effects of these measures can be quite profound in terms of traction and splintage and would have every expectation of improving the situation. And the earlier it is put on, the less blood you're going to effectively lose."

Greaney then asked a question which summed up Dr Davies's position on how those three basic techniques might have saved Saffie's life. "So you might improve a situation which nonetheless is going to be one in which survival is impossible.

"Or by improving the situation, you might make survival possible. Or you might make it probable, or I suppose you might make it certain," he said. "Where are you on the spectrum if those measures had been taken in the City Room?"

"If those injuries had been treated as described that early in her treatment, actually we have used the word probably."

"You say you've used the word probable," Greaney said. "Obviously as a matter of language that means more likely than not that she would have survived. Is that what you mean by using that word?"

"Yes," Davies said.

It was an astonishing moment for the inquiry. And quite a staggering difference to the view of the blast wave expert panel.

'Can I just find out, is that the view of both of you?" Sir John Saunders asked.

"Yes," Dr Park said.

Saffie could have had those three basic treatments at any stage up to the point where she reached hospital, which would have improved her chances, they said. The sooner the treatments are carried out, the better the outcome, of course.

"If those measures had been taken at that stage in the ambulance, would they have improved, in your view, Saffie's prospects of survival?" Greaney asked.

"Yes, without a doubt," Davies said. "I think if you look at the timing, there's potentially a window of 20 minutes where those interventions could have been in place and acting before Saffie enters cardiac arrest."

Davies said that if she had those interventions in the ambulance, she would probably still have survived.

Park said that it was "possible" she would have survived, but dropped her level of certainty down from "probably" because of the time lost without intervention.

By the time she reached hospital without those interventions, the odds were "stacked against her", said Davies. "I think it was likely that she'd die, yes, you could say that," he told the room. "The chances are stacked against her at that point, but not impossible."

"Not impossible, but stacked against her," said Greaney. "And Dr Park, do you agree with that assessment when we get to the hospital?"

"Yes," she confirmed, "I think she has a small chance of survival, but it's not beyond the chances of survival."

Davies said the situation called for a resuscitative

thoracotomy – which would mean opening her chest in that moment to identify the problems within. He said the doctors in the hospital, who decided not to try, should have tried, in his opinion.

"I think the decision was made on the basis that the injuries were unsurvivable and I think it is very, very hard to look at a patient in a matter of a few seconds and minutes to bring yourself to that position," Davies said.

Park agreed. They should have tried, in her opinion. Both had known patients with similar injuries who had the procedure and were saved.

There was no suggestion from either of them there were any issues with the competence or the dedication of any of the doctors or paramedics who tried to help Saffie that night. These were difficult calls to make, under extreme pressure, and in the moment.

But they were both clear. Early measures to stop the bleeding would have probably saved Saffie.

It had been a long week of tough evidence. Sir John was now faced with making a choice between the opinions of two sets of distinguished experts who disagreed, which was not an ideal situation to find himself in.

Andrew and Lisa were confident of one thing. Serious questions had now been raised about the blast wave experts' verdict that Saffie had no chance of surviving. Davies and Park did not agree.

And neither did Saffie's parents.

Chapter 31
Secrets and Lies

A few weeks before Saffie's evidence, Manchester was visited by a quite extraordinary person. You might walk past him in the street and not give him a second glance. But his work was some of the most secret in the UK, focusing on threats to our national security. He would describe his job as being like a "spider at the centre of a web".

His identification could see him or his family members targeted by terrorists or a hostile nation, such as Russia or China. He would make a perfect target for a Russian FSB sting, as part of their constant hunt for "kompromat", or damaging material, which can be used for blackmail purposes.

Witness J, as he must be known for legal and security purposes, was one of Britain's top spies – a senior MI5 officer close to the very top of the organisation, which is tasked with keeping the country safe from terrorism and foreign countries who would wish to undermine the UK and its democratic systems. Even the staff working at the inquiry would not know his name or identifying details, such was his security level.

He was to provide evidence behind a screen at the inquiry so that only Sir John Saunders, the inquiry chair, Paul Greaney, counsel to the inquiry, and lead advocates, such as Pete Weatherby, could see him. That way, at least, it could be confirmed there was a physical person in the room providing evidence.

Witness J entered the inquiry room by a non-public route. The hearing room was cleared and the secure camera feed into the courtroom was switched off. All electronic devices in the main hearing room had to be switched off except for the devices used by the official transcribers in the room and those needed for the inquiry's document management system.

The only recording of the evidence you are about to read was the official transcripts of the hearings. Any breach of these security measures would mean imprisonment for those responsible.

Witness J's evidence marked the beginning of the inquiry's look at whether the arena attack could and should have been prevented by the authorities. This would mean looking at what intelligence or information was available before the attack.

Was Salman Abedi investigated properly? Or had MI5 failed in their duty to protect the nation?

After all, Abedi had planned the attack over a six-month period, which had involved renting properties, purchasing a vehicle, acquiring large amounts of chemicals, and the manufacturing and securing of the explosives. There had been plenty of opportunities to gather evidence over the course of his plot.

MI5 and the Home Office had already argued that the

most important information would have to be heard in private for national security purposes. Sir John would be able to see the secret information, then a "gist", or summary, would be provided to the public.

The families were not happy. Andrew and Lisa would have liked more information to fall into the public domain, to avoid any possibility of a cover up.

But it was the best which could be managed, in the face of the battery of government lawyers who argued that secrecy and the national interest go hand in hand. MI5 will always be concerned about giving too much information away about its techniques to terrorists who might want to harm the UK.

There was a balance to be struck between the competing interests of open justice and accountability in a free and democratic society, with arguments about national security. After all, what is the point of defending democracy unless we live in one in the first place?

Where failings had been made, they could not be made in a secure building behind a locked door. The public have a right to know about such mistakes. Abedi's attack had slipped through the net, and the families wanted to know why. No cover ups, no manipulating the public narrative, just the truth.

Some efforts had already been made to understand whether there was anything to be learned from the attack. In 2018, the Intelligence and Security Committee of Parliament published a report entitled: "The 2017 attacks:

What needs to change". The security service and counter-terrorism police conducted their own internal reviews.

Those reviews where overseen by David Anderson QC, whose findings have already been covered by this book. Anderson concluded the attack might have been averted "had the cards fallen differently".

The public inquiry would now conduct its own independent investigation – taking into account all the information available to it, which was considerably more than previously.

But there was a big difference between the public inquiry and what had happened before. Sir John would have direct access to interview Witness J, as well as the intelligence officers who had handled the secret information about Salman Abedi.

Witness J was sworn in.

"Are you the witness who will be known as Witness J during the course of these proceedings?" asked Paul Greaney.

"Yes, I am."

"Have you been employed by MI5 for a period of now nearly 30 years?"

"Yes, I have."

"During that period have you held a number of different roles?"

"Yes, I have."

"Including being the director of a number of branches of MI5, spanning operational policy and work of analysis?"

"Yes, I did."

"At the time that you made your own witness statement, in May of 2020, were you the acting director-general of strategy for MI5?" Greaney asked.

"Yes."

"In that capacity were you one of three director generals working to support the overall director general?"

"Yes."

Witness J said his job had changed since May 2020. He was now director of the counter-terrorism section of MI5.

"A number of difficulties arise where detail is put into the public domain which relates to how MI5's capabilities have been used in operations. Is that correct?" Greaney asked.

"That's right," said J.

"Why is that so?"

" ... the more that we are describing how we operate against terrorists, the easier it is for them to hide their activities from us," J said. "Clearly, as an organisation seeking to protect the public, working alongside the police, we want to do our absolute best to disrupt terrorist activities without giving them opportunities to understand how we work against them."

This included giving away information about agents – who are members of the public providing the intelligence services with information – or information gathering techniques from, for example, intercepted communications.

MI5 had been under huge demand in the period leading up to the arena bomb, J said. The inquiry heard that the scale was "unprecedented" in terms of the number of current investigations and overall number of "subjects of interest", which meant people being actively investigated.

"At that stage, we're told MI5 was running about 500 investigations into individuals or groups associated with Islamist terrorism?" Greaney said.

"Yes."

"At the time of the arena attack, MI5 had around 3,000 active subjects of interest on its radar?"

"Yes."

"And was that on top of a larger pool of closed subjects of interest?" This meant people who had previously been investigated who were not currently being investigated.

"Yes," J said. "There were approximately at that time 20,000 closed subjects of interest."

The number was roughly equivalent to the population size of a small to medium-sized town, such as Reigate, Ascot, Market Harborough or Newquay.

The biggest threat was people who had travelled to Syria, Iraq and the surrounding region. There were around 850 such people, J said. Around half of them had returned to the UK. " ... significant effort and resource was required to deal with those 850, wherever they were located," J said.

He said a regional assessment of Manchester had been carried out in 2010. It had found a high level of discontentment within some Muslims across the city, which might influence the area's susceptibility to extremism. Many of them were young men whose parents had fled

Colonel Gaddafi in Libya in the 90s, to be taken in by the UK, and provided with homes and the freedom to practice their religion. They had settled in south Manchester, in an area known by some as "Little Tripoli".

"In short, therefore, there was identified to be an issue in Manchester with Islamist extremism?" Greaney said.

"Yes."

MI5 first received information about Salman Abedi on 30 December, 2010, shortly before his 16th birthday. MI5 was watching a particular subject of interest – who cannot be named – and Abedi had shared an address with that same person.

In December 2013, Abedi was on MI5's radar, being identified as a possible candidate for an unknown person who was observed acting suspiciously with a different subject of interest, who wanted to travel to Syria. It was a case of mistaken identity. The person observed with the suspect did not turn out to be Abedi.

MI5 were concerned that Abedi was speaking to extremists on the telephone. He was made a live subject of interest for seven months, then the investigation was shut down. He was moved from the pool of 3,000 people being actively investigated, into the larger pool of 20,000 people, who were no longer under direct observation.

In 2015, Abedi once again came to MI5's attention. He was identified as being the owner of a telephone number which had been in contact with an extremist linked to al-Qaeda. MI5 had information that Abedi had met with that person a number of times. But simply being in contact with that person was not considered enough to investigate him again.

"We have to make very fine judgements about whether somebody reaches a threshold for investigation and it can't just be on the basis of contact (with an extremist)," J said. "It has to be on the basis of more than that to ensure that we are making good decisions about how we use our resources …"

Later in 2015, MI5 received information Abedi was in contact with yet another person under their radar, who had been part of an extremist group in Libya. That person was judged to have played a part in radicalising Abedi.

On a single day in October 2015, Abedi was reopened and closed as a live subject of interest.

"This was based on a misunderstanding of information held by MI5 that indicated Salman Abedi's links to a senior Islamic State figure in Libya," said J.

MI5 received information on three more occasions that he was in contact with people on their watchlist, including one just a month before the attack, in April 2017.

Despite this, at no point was Abedi ever recommended by MI5 for the Prevent scheme, which is the government's strategy to stop people becoming terrorists or supporting terrorism.

Abedi was also in contact with a convicted extremist who he would visit in Belmarsh Prison and Liverpool Prison, as recently as 18 January, 2017. The pair had communicated regularly on the phone, shared more than 1,000 text messages. In the text messages there were references to martyrdom, the maidens of paradise, and a senior figure within Al-Qaeda.

"Is it correct that MI5 held information that indicated that Salman Abedi had visited a known extremist prisoner on more than one occasion?" Greaney asked.

"Yes, it is."

"In respect of the first visit, did MI5 ... actively seek information on the nature of Abedi's visit to that prisoner?"

"Yes."

MI5 still decided not to investigate Abedi. "I think it was a reasonable judgement to not open him as a subject of interest at the time on the basis of the contact with an extremist prisoner," J said. "There wasn't intelligence to indicate that the contact related to a threat to national security."

Greaney then moved on to perhaps the most important part of the evidence relating to MI5. "On two separate occasions in the months prior to the attack, was intelligence received by MI5 about Salman Abedi?" he asked.

"Yes."

"Was the significance of that intelligence not fully appreciated by MI5 at the time?"

"It wasn't," J said.

"At the time, what was it assessed to relate to?"

"At the time it was assessed to relate not to terrorism but to possible non-nefarious or to non-terrorist criminality on the part of Salman Abedi." In other words, MI5 thought Abedi could be up to no good, but he wasn't a terrorist.

"But does MI5 accept that in retrospect, the intelligence can be seen to have been highly relevant to the planned attack?" Greaney said.

"Yes."

The information, whatever it was, had not been shared with counter-terrorism police in the North West. It was MI5's job to assess the intelligence, and counter-terrorism police's job to act on it. In this case there had been a communication breakdown between the two organisations.

J said that he would be able to provide more details about that intelligence to Sir John Saunders behind closed doors.

"In closed, I can share in full detail the nature of that intelligence and the decisions that were made in response to it," J said. "This was fragments of the picture that we had at the time, but looking back, we can see that it was intelligence that was highly relevant to the planned attack."

Greaney took a moment, then asked one of the most important questions of the entire two-and-a-half-year inquiry.

"At the time, so not applying hindsight," Greaney said, "is it the view of MI5 that the decision that was made on the basis of that information not to re-open Salman Abedi was a reasonable judgement to make?"

"Yes, I think it was reasonable to make the judgement that this was assessed not to relate to terrorism, and it was reasonable to not open an investigation in response."

In March 2017, Abedi was one of 685 people who were closed subjects but were being looked at with a fresh pair of eyes by MI5 using something called "The Clematis process". Clematis was an attempt by MI5 to sift through the pool of 20,000 for any signs of people who were re-engaging in extremist behaviour.

On 1 May, Abedi's case was assessed under Clematis and it was decided he met the threshold for further investigation. At that point MI5 discovered he was in Libya, not Manchester.

On 8 May, so two weeks before the attack, the Clematis team assessed that Abedi should be considered for low-level investigative inquiries to be carried out in order to identify if he had re-engaged in Islamist extremist activity. This type of low-level investigation into closed subjects of interest was known within MI5 circles as the "Daffodil process".

Clematis would sift through the closed cases for any signs of renewed extremist activity, and anyone who showed signs of risk would be referred to the Daffodil team for investigation. This is how MI5 works. It receives information, assesses that intelligence, and assigns resources which it deems proportional to the risk.

Abedi was one of 26 people due to be considered for referral into the Daffodil process at a meeting which had been scheduled for 31 May – nine days after the bomb.

Abedi flew into Manchester Airport on 18 May, four days before his attack. He had been recommended for referral into the Daffodil process, yet no ports action had been placed on him following his travel to Libya in April. It meant he was not stopped and searched when he returned to the UK.

MI5's review team, which looked for learning points after the attack, concluded that stopping the plot would have been "unlikely" at this stage. "Does it follow that you agree with that conclusion?" Greaney asked.

"Yes, it does," J said.

Sir John asked how the MI5 review team could say stopping the attack was unlikely, had the ports action had been put in place. What if the police had searched him, downloaded his phone, and found instructions on how to make a bomb?

J said MI5 would not have asked police to treat the case as a priority. " ... because he was a closed subject of interest, someone who we didn't have indications of attack planning," he said.

The team which would have investigated Abedi was also extremely busy at the time, said J. "In particular in May 2017 there were a substantial number of live and suspended investigations both within MI5 generally and within the team that would have been responsible for investigating Salman Abedi."

J said in the four days between Abedi returning to the UK and carrying out his attack, it would have been difficult to stop him. Abedi took steps to avoid the detection of his activity.

MI5 struggled to obtain intelligence on him while he was

in Libya, which was possibly why he chose to go there in the lead-up. It is also possible he was receiving instructions on how to carry out the attack. The preparations for the bomb device had already been made. The home-made explosives and other materials were waiting for him in a boot of a car in Rusholme, outside his friend's apartment.

There were only a few steps left to make the bomb, including making the trigger device.

Since the attack, J said the security service now ran more checks under Clematis than before the arena bomb, which meant sifting through the pool of closed subjects of interest more often. This was a major learning point for MI5 after the attack. They now use more resources to check the pool of 20,000 people more often.

Andrew and Lisa were appalled. Why had it taken the murder of 22 people for them to update their computer system?

Sir John was incredulous that Abedi had never been referred to the government's Prevent scheme. " ... you knew that since the age of 15 he had been in contact with people who may radicalise," he told J. "So from a fairly young age, when he was a subject of interest, when he was 18 or 19, you knew that he had been in contact with some fairly serious people within terrorism.

"You knew about his father having been involved in terrorist activity in Libya. Doesn't he just look like an obvious candidate for somebody who might be being dragged into terrorism?

" ... just looking at those basic facts, he ought to have been referred to Prevent. I can't say it would have made any difference, nor can you, it's speculation, but this was a government programme designed to prevent radicalisation and MI5 didn't take advantage of it."

J took a moment to respond. "I have seen the real value of Prevent in cases in the past where somebody has those risk factors that you're referring to," he admitted. "From an MI5 perspective, when we closed Salman Abedi in 2014, he was one of a group of 20,000 closed subject of interests, so there needs to be some clear judgements around who you would refer and why. In 2014 when we closed him, I see very little basis for us referring him to Prevent based on the intelligence picture we had at the time."

J remained adamant it was a reasonable decision by MI5.

Greaney had finished his questions. Now it was the turn of John Cooper QC, a barrister who, like Weatherby, represented a number of the families. Cooper was like a firework, ready to ignite. The families wanted answers, not excuses, not avoidance of the questions due to vague claims about national security. They wanted the truth.

"Just getting to the crux of this," Cooper said, "and we'll go into more detail in a moment, would you accept for all the caveats that you have given us, that MI5 failed to identify a bomber who went on to kill 22 people on 22 May 2017?"

"Mr Cooper ... before I answer that question, which I will do, can I just express my personal condolences on behalf of myself and MI5 to those who lost family members and loved ones in the attack and to all those who were injured or affected by the events of that day," J said.

Cooper thanked him. But said it was his duty to press him on this matter, on behalf of the families, who had waited a long time for the opportunity to hear from MI5.

Cooper asked him the question again.

"Yes," J said. "We exist to protect the public and to keep this country safe and so when an attack like this happens, of course we're acknowledging that we haven't been able to do that. As an organisation, and personally, I'm so sorry that we didn't stop this.

"My job over the past few months has been to identify whether or not there were moments where we did fail, in your language, moments where we should have done things that would have prevented this attack. But I haven't detected failure in my analysis of this.

"I've detected areas where, looking back, of course with the benefit of hindsight, there were different decisions that could have been made."

Sir John interjected. "Witness J, I hope you don't mind me saying so, there may be good reasons for it, but I think the answer to the question has to be yes, doesn't it? MI5 did not identify Salman Abedi before the attack took place."

"Yes. So we failed to identify in that language that he was going to conduct this attack."

Cooper was not happy with the response. He pushed further. " ... As a general principle – we'll work on why, but as a general proposition, surely it's one of the most straightforward questions I'm going to ask you today? MI5 failed to protect those families from a bomber? Failed."

"We live in a society where, unfortunately, despite our work and the work of others, terrorist attacks do happen," J said. "And it's a very uncomfortable and horrible thing to say but that is the case. And in these circumstances, yes, we didn't identify that he was planning this attack, and we didn't stop him, quite self-evidently. So yes, MI5 didn't ..."

"Come on, say it, *failed?*" Cooper said.

"I think he has already answered that," Sir John intervened.

Cooper moved on. He asked whether MI5 was underfunded. Under-resourced. J said it had no impact on the Abedi attack. Cooper said that MI5 should have been on high alert to Abedi because of his father, Ramadan, and his own extremist views.

J said that Abedi was almost certainly influenced by his father. But he could say no more in "open" evidence.

"MI5 knew that and knew that well before 2017, didn't they? Surely you can answer that question?"

"Again Mr Cooper, I can't in open."

"You are trying to help us here, Witness J?" Cooper asked.

"He has told you," Sir John said to Cooper. "It may be justified or not, the question of national security, but that's something I will look at."

Cooper suggested J was using national security as an excuse not to answer questions. J, of course, denied this.

J returned for a second day of "open" evidence. It was now Pete Weatherby's chance to interrogate one of MI5's most senior officers. Andrew and Lisa wanted Weatherby to explore something they believed was a key question.

How was he allowed to leave the UK for Libya to return four days later without being stopped?

Weatherby described how Abedi arrived into Manchester Airport, where he went to buy a SIM card for his mobile phone, then got on a bus, and after that a taxi. He was showing evidence of counter-surveillance techniques, getting two forms of transport.

Weatherby suggested that either stopping him at the border or following him from the airport might have stopped the attack. "So ports action might have stopped him doing what he was going to do ... or it could conceivably have led to something in his property or something he said or indeed being followed to the bomb, yes?"

"Conceivably, yes," J answered.

After checking on the bomb parts and explosives in the car boot in Rusholme, Abedi then went to a flat in an apartment block he had rented on the edge of the city centre, close to the Gay Village He finished making the bomb, visiting a DIY shop to purchase bags of metal nuts and bolts to pack into the device.

" ... if in fact he had been stopped by the police (at the airport), putting that together, there is a significant chance it would have stopped him carrying out his plot, isn't there?" Weatherby said.

J said they would have needed a high priority investigation to be following him around at that time.

" ... it's certainly possible that you would have observed slightly unusual behaviour at the airport or beyond the airport and then followed it on and, as I say, it would have led you to the bomb?" Weatherby asked, in his usual assured tone.

"To be clear on the question about what we knew, we had fragments of what we now know to be the picture, so the post-incident investigation and all of the material that was obtained from that gives you that trail, but we had a blurred picture at that time of Salman Abedi and we did not conclude that the intelligence we had related to attack planning," J said.

Abedi went on reconnaissance trips to the arena before his attack, during which time he was showing knowledge of anti-surveillance techniques, J said.

Weatherby pressed the point. Questioning J, one of the UK's top spies, was like pushing against a brick wall.

If he was stopped at the airport and questioned, it might have prevented the attack, Weatherby said.

J said it was speculation.

"I'm slightly baulking at the word 'speculation'," Weatherby said. "There is evidence that he was interested in you not knowing what he was up to?"

"But that doesn't take us to the point where a port stop would have deterred him or changed his behaviour necessarily," J said.

"Ok, I have made my point," Weatherby said.

Weatherby asked if a port stop had even been considered – given that information had been received weeks before about Abedi. J refused to answer if it had been considered. He said it related to the overall intelligence picture which would be disclosed in closed evidence.

"I do want to be helpful," J insisted, "I'm not trying to avoid the question about whether or not we considered or there was a judgement around it. But it is directly relevant to the intelligence picture we had at the time in terms of the decisions that were made and the judgements that were made based on that."

Then, a breakthrough. J conceded that Abedi should have been subject to a port stop.

"We concluded that a better course of action would have been to put him on port stop," J said.

They should have stopped him at the border. And by doing so, Weatherby pointed out, they might have stopped the attack from happening in the first place.

Chapter 32
The Northwest Station

MI5 has stations based in various locations around the UK, outside of its headquarters in London, all working to disrupt and prevent terror attacks from extremists. The Northwest Station, whose location is top-secret, was one of its busiest. Counter-terrorism police officers were also based there, too, supposed to work side by side with MI5 staff, but their computer systems for sharing information were clunky and outdated. In the months leading up to the Manchester bombing, intelligence was falling through the gaps.

The inside story of MI5's Northwest Station was heard during the inquiry's final day of evidence on 15 February, 2022.

In April 2017, a month before the attack, the investigative team based at the station went into "amber" on its workload dashboard. This meant it was in a period of stress and high demand. Work had to be distributed to some of the other regional teams. Some of the Northwest Station's investigations had to be suspended in order to keep up. By May 2017 they were receiving assistance from other parts of MI5, but the benefit of that assistance had not yet been felt.

This was a world away from the picture sketched out by

Witness J in his own evidence, when he had claimed that resources played no part in the failures to catch Abedi. The station which would have been tasked with an investigation was in fact struggling to cope.

There were concerns in intelligence circles about the Libyan community in south Manchester. Specifically, they perceived a risk that the younger generations were becoming more attracted to al-Qaeda influenced extremism as they lost the nationalist focus of their parents.

After the murder of Fusilier Lee Rigby in 2013, MI5 was more focused on lone actors. Their behavioural science unit was helping to assess subjects of interest to work out if they had the potential to carry out similar lone attacks.

At the same time, the Northwest Station was especially busy due to Manchester's large Libyan population. Libya was one of MI5's top priorities.

The US had carried out bombing raids on Islamic State targets in Libya in early 2017. Islamic State had responded by saying that Europe was a target for terrorist attacks. Separately to this, the UK national threat level, set by the Joint Terrorism Analysis Centre and MI5 itself, was "severe" in May 2017, meaning an attack was highly likely. This was the second highest of five categories.

A piece of research by counter-terrorism police the year before had examined travellers from Manchester to Libya over a period of three months, looking at fighting age boys and men aged 16 to 30 years.

The outcome was that there were 544 such individuals.

Counter-terrorism policing was engaging with mosques in south Manchester, but Didsbury Mosque did not respond positively to the contact, according to one senior police officer. It was the same mosque attended by the Abedi family.

Islamic State propaganda was flooding social media, and it had become "cool" amongst certain groups in the Libya community of Manchester to take an interest. It was becoming wrapped up in a sub-culture of drugs, gangster rap, and cannabis.

The information about the Northwest Station emerged on the last day as part of the summary of closed evidence. The 10 days of closed hearings – which happened over November 2021 – also considered the two pieces of intelligence MI5 received about Abedi shortly before the attack.

What was that intelligence, exactly? A warning from a source at Didsbury mosque? A tip-off from one of Abedi's friends? Or had MI5 managed to intercept some communications which hinted at what was to come? Maybe some clue about the chemical purchases on Amazon? It was a mystery, which endures to this day.

Listening to the closed evidence was Sir John Saunders, the inquiry's legal team, Home Office lawyers, GMP lawyers, and members of the northwest's counter-terrorism unit. Four MI5 witnesses provided evidence, alongside ten counter-terrorism police officers.

Paul Greaney read out a 15-page document containing

"the gist". It revealed details about the MI5 Regional Station covering the northwest, where there had been a significant increase in workload from 2015. One officer at the station had complained about it.

"He had raised with his superiors his concerns regarding the triaging of intelligence and was worried something could get through due to the volumes of documents they were considering," Greaney said.

This was a very different picture to Witness J claiming that resources had not been an issue in missing the arena bomber.

And there were more revelations.

The Northwest Station had limited time to consider wider leads and work and manage intelligence in relation to closed subjects of interest – like Salman Abedi, it was heard. The computer system they had for triaging new information was not as effective as it could have been. One of the MI5 witnesses said it would take two weeks to assess new information coming in. Their systems for receiving such information were "a bit haphazard", the inquiry heard.

MI5 and the police had different systems for intelligence sharing because of questions around protecting sensitive information. The systems were so poor that electronic files would not transfer properly between the two organisations if the file size was too large. Some PowerPoint presentations, for example, had to be sent slide by slide between MI5 and the police.

There is no record of either of the two pieces of

intelligence received in the months prior to the attack about Abedi being shared by MI5 with counter-terrorism police.

Sir John had heard the full truth about that intelligence. And his final report, which was due to be published the following year, would cause shockwaves throughout the intelligence community.

For now, though, the inquiry was over.

Once again, the names of those who died were read out loud. The families didn't know it yet, but MI5 had downplayed their evidence to the inquiry. The attack could have been stopped. And they were going to find out why.

Chapter 33
Moments in Time

In November 2022, Andrew and Lisa were contacted by their legal team and warned that the inquiry's emergency services report was about to come out. The report had found a catalogue of failings and mistakes by the emergency services. Much of it they knew already. It was the findings about Saffie which concerned them most.

Pete Weatherby, Nicola Brook, and Elkan Abrahamson rang them up the day the report was published to the general public. They had received a summary of the findings a few hours before they were going to released at 2pm.

Sir John had noted there had been "significant disagreement" between the blast wave panel of experts and "some of the additional experts I instructed" in relation to Saffie.

"The former ultimately considered that there was no possibility that Saffie-Rose Roussos would have survived whatever treatment she had received. The latter felt that survival was not an impossibility with the best treatment," Sir John said.

Sir John weighed the evidence and considered that the blast wave panel of experts had been right about the nature and extent of the injuries suffered by Saffie, in terms of the injuries to her legs and her lungs. "That does not mean, however, that the final conclusion of the blast wave panel of experts that survival was impossible is correct," Sir John found in his report.

"Even though I accept that the blast wave panel were right about the nature and extent of the injuries, I do not consider that the evidence enables me to say that she had absolutely no chance of survival if the most comprehensive and advanced medical treatment had been initiated immediately after injury."

He said that Dr Gareth Davies and Lieutenant Colonel Park were experienced and impressive experts. "Their evidence about what consultants in pre-hospital emergency medicine can achieve out of hospital was striking. The evidence of their experiences means that I cannot exclude the remote possibility that Saffie-Rose Roussos would have survived ..."

Sir John said she would have had a chance of survival if she had received treatment from an experienced consultant in pre-hospital emergency medicine immediately, followed by swift evacuation to hospital and expert treatment there. However, he described her as having a "remote possibility of survival".

He had overruled the blast wave panel that their daughter had "nil" chance of survival. But Andrew and Lisa have never fully accepted Sir John's findings. They could not.

In their view, Davies and Park were the experts in this

field. They said Saffie would probably have lived, had she been given three basic medical interventions. Saunder's report did nothing to persuade Andrew and Lisa otherwise.

Lisa felt angry. If Saffie had at least been given the interventions that Davies and Park had recommended, and then not survived, she could understand where the blast wave experts were coming from. But Saffie had never even received a tourniquet. How could they say she had no chance of survival?

Andrew was frustrated at the language used by Sir John in his report, saying that Saffie had a "remote" possibility of survival. He could not understand where the word "remote" had come from, since it had not been used by either blast wave panel, or Davies and Park.

Saffie was a fighter with a big heart and a strong spirit. She had fought for her life for 69 minutes after the bomb exploded.

She had the awareness to have asked a paramedic: "Am I going to die?" That told Andrew and Lisa something. It told them she was still fighting, and had awareness of her surroundings.

They believed, more than anything, that she should have lived, if she had been given the help she needed.

*

Andrew and Lisa felt deflated. They had wanted to get to the truth about Saffie. They had gone into the inquiry not knowing anything about what happened to her after the bomb. They had decided to listen to every detail of the inquiry in order to advocate for their daughter.

The opinion of the blast wave panel had changed, and the second opinion was completely different. For Lisa it was like mental torture.

Where did that leave them with the truth?

The third and final report by Sir John was published in March 2023, and covered how the arena bomber had been radicalised, and whether MI5 could have stopped the attack.

Abedi had left no message to explain his reasons for the arena bomb. There has never been a definitive answer, although his brother suggested they were supporters of Islamic State. Knowing their motives meant little to Andrew or Lisa.

What MI5 knew before the attack and whether or not they should have stopped it was far more important. The families wanted to know if they had done their job properly.

Sir John had been given an advantage that the other previous reviews did not. He had been given direct access to three MI5 officers who directly handled the intelligence about Abedi before the attack took place. Sir John was able to question them under oath.

Could Salman Abedi have been stopped before he carried out his attack at the Ariana Grande concert? In March 2023, Sir John published the answer in his third and final report.

Outside Manchester Magistrates' Court, journalists and TV crews gathered to get ready. Some reporters had been allowed to go inside to read the report ahead of publication as part of a "lock in", but they were not allowed to contact their news organisations about the contents before Sir John gave a summary of the findings at 2pm.

Manchester had changed since the attack. People had come together, but there was a wariness which existed for a long time after about large public events. The city was famous for its music. For the terror attack to have struck at a music concert felt like an attack on the culture and fabric of the city itself.

Just before Sir John announced his findings, there was a minute's silence to remember those who died. Sir John then began his press conference.

"I have found a significant missed opportunity to take action that might have prevented the attack," he said. "It is not possible to reach any conclusion on the balance of probabilities or to any other evidential standard as to whether the attack would have been prevented. However, there was a realistic possibility that actionable intelligence could have been obtained which might have led to action preventing the attack.

"The reason for this missed opportunity included a failure by the security service, in my view, to act swiftly enough."

His report revealed the following.

In the months prior to the attack, MI5 received two pieces of intelligence about Abedi: intelligence 1 and intelligence 2.

Witness J stated in his open evidence: "At the time, it (both pieces of intelligence) was assessed to relate not to terrorism but to possible non-nefarious activity or to non-terrorist criminality on the part of Salman Abedi."

Anderson himself had also found this, based on what MI5 had told him at the time, during his post-attack reviews. In an interview aired by the BBC in a Panorama programme broadcast in 2022, he said: "MI5 admitted to me at least two things they got wrong.

"And the first thing was that when, early in 2017, they received intelligence and they interpreted it as to do probably with drugs or organised crime and not something to do with terrorism or national security."

Sir John wrote in his report: "Having heard from those witnesses who handled piece of intelligence 1 and piece of intelligence 2, I do not consider that these statements present an accurate picture."

The corporate position of MI5 did not match what its own intelligence officers had told Sir John. Sir John had directly interviewed an MI5 officer, known only as Witness C. Witness C had never been spoken to before about the intelligence by any previous review.

This was why Sir John had such an advantage. He could ask Witness C questions under oath, and get their response directly, rather than through MI5's corporate filter. Neither piece of intelligence was shared by MI5 with counter-terrorism police.

The detail of what the intelligence was has never been

disclosed to the public for national security reasons. In the case of piece of intelligence 1, Witness C had wondered whether it might have some national security significance "that merited further investigation", Sir John said.

If it was received today, based on current policy, it would have opened Salman Abedi up to low-level investigative inquiries, in conjunction with the police.

Two other MI5 officers who Sir John was able to interview – Witness A and Witness B – both said that if further context had been provided by Witness C in their report about piece of intelligence 1, then it might have led to further investigative steps being taken at the time.

"I accept that Witness C, who first assessed piece of intelligence 1, was genuinely seeking to pass on what she/he considered to be useful," Sir John said.

"However, in my view, they should have provided further context. Had Witness C done so, it is likely that further low-level investigative steps would have been taken in relation to Salman Abedi at the time. Witness C's assessment of piece of intelligence 1 at the time was that it might have some national security significance."

Witness C was also the security service officer who first assessed piece of intelligence 2. "Witness C gave compelling evidence that when they assessed piece of intelligence 2 they had in mind the possibility of activity of pressing national security concern. In my view, they were right to.

"Given that Witness C had that in mind, they should have discussed it with the other security service officers straight away. Moreover, they should have written the report on the same day, but in fact did not do so. In the context of national security, if there is a need to do something it is usually necessary to do it promptly."

Witness J and MI5 supported that officer's approach in terms of the timing of their report. Sir John disagreed. The report had not been provided as promptly as it should have.

Witness A and Witness B were also of the view that if further context had been given in the report on piece of intelligence 2 and received prior to 22 May, 2017, then it might have led to further investigative steps being taken.

Sir John agreed that the report written by Witness C had not been good enough. The delay in C providing the report on piece of intelligence 2 meant an opportunity had been missed to gather intelligence on Abedi. "Based on everything the security service knew or should have known, I am satisfied that such an investigation action would have been a proportionate and justified step to take. This should have happened," he found.

If that action had been taken, Sir John said it was impossible to say on the balance of probabilities if the attack would have been stopped. But it might have led to Abedi being followed after arriving at Manchester Airport, which would have led MI5 to his car containing the explosives and bomb parts.

A port stop at the airport might also have deterred his plot. "There is a possibility that he had the switch for the bomb on him at that time," Sir John said.

MI5 had painted an inaccurate picture of the intelligence they had received before the arena bomb. "It became apparent," Sir John found, "that the security service's corporate position did not reflect what those officers did, thought or would have done at the material time."

MI5's own officers disagreed with the organisation's public position on the intelligence – that it was assessed as criminal, but not national security or terror related. That simply was not true, said Witness C, who had personally handled that intelligence.

Sir John's conclusions were devastating. He said the attack might have been prevented. But he also rejected MI5's assessment that Salman and Hashem were alone in carrying out the plot. He believed they had received help in Libya shortly before Salman returned.

Many of the families were angry. Some made statements outside the courtroom in front of the media. Richard Scorer, principal lawyer of law firm Slater and Gordon, read out a statement representing 11 victims' families.

The families had been deeply affected by the information that there had been a delay in reporting on the intelligence about Abedi. "This is a devastating conclusion for us," they said.

They said the failures exposed in the report were unacceptable, and that the public was entitled to expect that information of national security importance is acted on quickly. They were "failed at every level before, during and after this attack," said the families.

Suella Braverman, who by then was Home Secretary, issued a statement on behalf of the government. "I am committed to working with MI5, policing and partners to study the recommendations. Together we will do everything possible to prevent a repeat of this horrifying attack," she said.

Sir John said a scheme needed to be created to prevent extremist prisoners from radicalising those who visit them. He said the Department for Education should consider whether schools should include notes of significant behavioural problems on records which follow a student when they move school. And that the government strengthens legislation on witnesses that are not complying with inquiries, such as Ismail Abedi, who fled the country.

The report demanded a response from MI5. That day, Ken McCallum, the director general of MI5, issued an unprecedented public apology.

"Having examined all the evidence, the chair of the inquiry found that there was a realistic possibility that actionable intelligence could have been obtained which might have led to actions preventing the attack. I deeply regret that such intelligence was not obtained.

"Gathering covert intelligence is difficult – but had we managed to seize the slim chance we had, those impacted might not have experienced such appalling loss and trauma. I am profoundly sorry that MI5 did not prevent the attack."

A "slim chance". This was not the language used by the final conclusions of the public inquiry.

Andrew and Lisa had made emotional appeals from the witness box for the authorities to be open and honest about what happened. They felt misled. In their view, MI5's obfuscation was disrespectful to Saffie and her memory.

The spider at the centre of the web had been caught out.

*

"They should have stopped it, and now knowing this just adds to it, to the point where, it's heart breaking," Andrew told BBC Newsnight. "Saffie is coming into my mind now and I'm thinking, 'Our country could have saved you'."

It was three weeks since Sir John had published his report, and MI5 issued their unprecedented apology. Newsnight had been approached by two intelligence sources with new details about what went wrong.

MI5 had received a specific intelligence lead naming Salman Abedi and linking him to a bomb plot before the attack, according to the BBC. BBC Newsnight claimed the mistake was so serious it could be regarded "negligent" in a court of law.

"Why did you not act on that information? That's what's going through my head right now," Andrew told the BBC. "You might turn around and say this is not strong enough information. But surely as MI5 you would think – 'ok if we look at our history, we have known this guy since 2010'."

Andrew was furious. "I can't swallow it. I can't. They need to take this information and admit to their failings."

The family began talking to Pete Weatherby, their barrister, about what further legal steps could be taken to reveal more about what MI5 knew about Abedi before the attack. Could a legal action be brought specifically against the security services? It had never been done before. The victims of a terror plot have never before sued MI5 for failing to stop an attack.

But just because it had never been done, does not necessarily mean it could not. Weatherby realised there was a possibility of bringing a human rights case in the Investigatory Powers Tribunal. The tribunal was a secretive affair. It heard human rights cases against MI5, MI6 and GCHQ. Much of the evidence it considered was secret. The case would come under Article 2 of the Human Rights Act, known as the right to life, the legislation which enshrines the European Convention on Human Rights into UK law.

That article says that the government should take appropriate measures to safeguard life by making laws to protect you and, in some circumstances, by taking steps to protect you if your life is at risk. MI5 had failed to do this, Weatherby argued.

Witness C had known there was a risk to national security after assessing the intelligence about Abedi. But appropriate steps had not been taken to protect the public. Sir John himself said they had missed a "significant opportunity" to prevent the attack.

Andrew wanted Weatherby and the law firm, Broudie Jackson Canter, to pursue the case. And he was not alone.

A group of more than 250 people are now part of the group action, being represented by three separate law firms. The legal action is not about money or compensation. This means little to the families. No amount of money could ever bring back their loved ones.

The legal action is about the pursuit of the truth. What was the intelligence MI5 received about Abedi? Why was it not acted upon? And had MI5 acted with candour at the public inquiry?

In November 2024, two judges presiding over the Investigatory Powers Tribunal heard the arguments from the families that the case should go ahead. Usually, claims had to be brought within 12 months of the incident itself, which, in this case, was the arena bomb in 2017. Pete Weatherby, on behalf of the families, argued this had not been possible, since MI5's failures were only fully known when Sir John Saunders delivered his final report in 2023. Only then did the families find out about, for example, the delay by an intelligence officer in passing on key information. It was unfair, Weatherby argued, to reject the claim based on such a timeframe.

MI5's lawyers pointed out the length of time since the incident before the claim had been brought. "The passage of time will inevitably reduce the cogency of witness evidence," they told the judges. MI5 argued there was no public interest in the claim, since it was unlikely that further information would be brought to light that had not been already heard in the public inquiry. MI5 said it had already spent considerable time and resources over many years co-operating with the investigations.

The claim would mean resource being diverted away from MI5, with senior figures required to "give instructions, allocate resources, and provide further evidence". The tribunal issued their judgement later that month, ruling in MI5's favour. The claim would not go ahead. It had not been brought in good time, said the judges, and it would require MI5 to divert resources from their responsibilities. "Those responsibilities of course include the protection of the lives of people in this country, for example, preventing future attacks," said the tribunal's ruling.

The claim would not proceed. And the questions about what MI5 really knew about Abedi before the attack would go unanswered.

*

Andrew and Lisa will never stop fighting. They believe they owe it to their daughter. Many of the families believe they owe a similar debt to their loved ones.

Their lives in Dorset are quieter now than those busy days in the shop in Leyland. They both prefer it that way. Lisa can walk along the street without a stick, Andrew holding her hand as they make their way along the promenade. They go to the gym regularly. Lisa swims, Andrew lifts free weights. The exercise helps with their mental wellbeing.

Xander, now 19, has finished college. He works as a shop assistant, and enjoys playing computer games with his friends. He has grown into a fine young man. He rarely speaks about Saffie and what happened. The pair used to be inseparable. Saffie was like Xander's shadow. He has to make his own way now, without her.

Ashlee is a regular visitor to their house with Ever-Rose, who is quickly growing up. Andrew and Lisa are doting grandparents. They take her on trips to their local beach, where she runs about on the sand and splashes in the sea. They take her swimming, and every night they will make her a little bed in their own home, to make sure she is safe. And just before they go to sleep every night, Ever-Rose will sing them nursery songs. Her favourite is Rain, Rain, Go Away, so she will wake up the next day in the sunshine and go to the beach.

The Sun newspaper launched Saffie's Smile awards, a competition designed to honour Saffie's memory, and celebrate young people aged 16 or under who go above and beyond to help others. "As a family, we wanted to do something positive, something uplifting and joyful," Andrew told the media. "Because that is who Saffie was. She was a very giving and loving child."

In July 2024, as part of the launch, they visited New York with Xander and Ashlee. Saffie's image was projected on the largest billboard screen in Times Square on 4 July, which would have been Saffie's 16th birthday.

They spent hours going through the different award

entries. They eventually chose Ruby Reid, who had helped her mother when she was suffering from a medical condition, doing the housework and looking after her.

Most days you will find Andrew and Lisa at home. They have called their house Saffie-Rose. Binky scuttles about, barking at people who knock on the door, or walk past the window. They bought a second dog, a pug called Obi, to give Binky some company. Andrew enjoys entertaining guests with his Greek barbecue, complete with an electric motor for turning the pork skewers. He has always loved cooking, and takes pleasure in making food for people.

Lisa still enjoys watching the waves. On a clear and sunny day, if you go to a certain beach in Dorset, you might just see Andrew and Lisa, holding hands, walking across the sands, Binky and Obi scampering by the shoreline. They will travel to Cyprus a few weeks of every year, where they will spend time with their family. They loved Saffie as much as she loved them. They find comfort in their happy memories of her.

Their mission in life is make sure that nobody ever forgets Saffie. They are the guardians of her life and her memory.

They are still learning how to live with their grief. There is not a single day which goes by when they do not think about her. Saffie-Rose Roussos. Made from love.

Epilogue

New York, Boxing Day, 2015

They had finally arrived. New York, at Christmas.

Saffie wasn't interested in unpacking everything neatly into the wardrobes and cupboards of their hotel room. She wanted to get out and see the sights. The giant Christmas tree at the Rockefeller Center. The ice skating at Central Park. The big statue of a lady holding a torch.

"Can we go, yet?" she asked her parents, lying with Xander on the queen-sized bed. Andrew and Lisa were sipping cocktails, looking out at the view of the Empire State Building from their bedroom window.

Saffie loved seeing cities at night. She loved the lights and the buzz of the streets. She liked the idea of being around lots of people. It felt exciting.

They left the hotel when the sun went down and walked along a side street. Saffie was pointing at everything and asking questions. Yellow taxis streamed past. People were talking on their phones in loud American accents. The buildings soared up into the night sky either side of the street, the windows in neat symmetrical rows.

It had been a tough three years. They had worked hard to make the fish and chip shop a success. It had meant working twelve hours a day, six days a week. It was the hardest they had ever worked in their entire lives.

The New York trip had been Andrew's idea. He wanted to treat the family. They had experienced poverty and come out the other side. Now it was time to create some memories.

Saffie was skipping down the street. She could never contain her excitement. You could see it in her body. She was a bundle of energy, constantly moving, never staying still.

They were about to reach their destination. "Come here," Andrew said to Saffie. "You walk in front of me. I'm just going to cover your eyes."

Saffie stood in front of her dad, and they walked together down the street, Andrew's hands over her eyes. She loved the suspense. They brushed past people on their way to the very centre of the square.

Andrew looked at Lisa. Lisa nodded, and Andrew took away his hands from Saffie's eyes. Saffie stood in the middle of Times Square.

The dazzling lights of the billboards reflected in her big brown eyes. Her expression changed from excitement and suspense to one of joy and wonder.

Andrew and Lisa will remember Saffie just like that, forever.

Andrew and Lisa Roussos: Acknowledgements

A public inquiry is a tough and challenging process. After two years of choosing not to know anything about Saffie we were forced to make a decision: either not to engage with the inquiry and let our legal team take care of it, or face it. Facing it would mean knowing every detail. But we both knew in the end we had to represent Saffie because we were her voice. Our book will take you through a roller-coaster of emotions and the true facts we had to endure.

There are a number of people we would like to thank. We would like to thank the NHS and the amazing work they do.

A special thank you to the doctors, nurses, surgeons and physios on the acute ICU at Wythenshawe Hospital who not only cared for Lisa around the clock but also the whole family, and nothing was ever too much. We will be forever grateful.

Thank you to the wonderful Professor Lees for everything she did and continues to do. You truly are a special person who we respect and appreciate more than our words can write. Thank you to Johnny Duncan, whose gentle bedside manner and upbeat personality never failed to put a smile on our faces.

Thank you to Mark Welch for saving Lisa's leg under the

immense pressure and the limited timeframe you were in. We are in awe.

And to Mr van Popta who removed the bolt from the top of Lisa's spine. Again, we will be forever grateful.

Thank you to all the ICU nurses who tended Lisa and supported the family. To Kate, who tirelessly took care of Lisa. To lovely Jo, who was always so kind and patient. To Sue, for putting up with Lisa's "thirst" tantrums, and helping us see the funny side of her delusions when she was "high" on medication. Thank you to beautiful nurse Rosie, who always showed us warmth and kindness.

And to Lorraine, our heartfelt thanks for always going above and beyond to do everything she could to help. You continue to give us love and support and we are honoured to call you our dearest friend.

Thank you to every single one of you from the bottom of our hearts. You are all with us and felt the true horror of that night. And you will all stay in our hearts forever.

Thank you to Lisa's brother Stephen and wife Janey. Stephen you never left my bedside, even though you were breaking inside. You held my hand and reassured me that you were always there. Thank you to Lisa's sister Karen and husband Jamie, for the care and support in the years that followed.

Thank you to Andrew's brother Chris, Pat and the girls, for always giving us a safe space. With you it feels like home. To our wonderful Cyprus family for their love, care and warmth.

Thank you to Lisa's dearest friend Dawn, for caring for Lisa in the hospital. You were there every day at 6am and the sound of your footsteps down the hospital corridor reassured Lisa she wasn't alone.

To dearest friend Sam, who has been Lisa's constant throughout. Lisa can never thank you enough for your emotional support being the best friend you can be.

What would Lisa do without you? To Janine, who is the sunshine to Lisa's soul. Thank you for making Lisa belly-laugh again.

To Paula for always loving Lisa. To big Nic, for making Lisa feel 16 again. To little Nic, for being so thoughtful, and to Dean for just being you. To Barbara, for always being there for Lisa and a listening ear.

To Karen Carlin, for taking Lisa's late-night calls. And for checking in on Lisa. And to husband Martin for organising a beautiful Saffie-Rose garden at the school.

To Chris Upton, Saffie's headteacher, for everything you have done, and are still doing, making the school a safe and happy place. Thank you to all the staff, pupils and parents, who all did their best in helping the school get through such a tragedy.

And so much love to Kate and Jess. You are both very special people. To Victim Support, and Krissy. What would we have done without you? Such an important charity.

Thank you to the community of Leyland who came together and showed us so much love and support, and to Jim, that hug in the church was everything.

The city of Manchester: You have supported and lifted us up every single day. Your love, strength and unity will live with us forever. You felt and shared our pain.

Thank you to people around the world who took Saffie into their hearts and sent us your love and support.

Thank you Mike and family. Nothing was ever too much. And Lily. Your love for Saffie was unconditional and she loved you very much.

To Nigel, at AW Lymn Rose, thank you for your kindness and generosity. It was greatly appreciated.

Thank you to Reverend Canon Marcia Wall of Manchester Cathedral, who showed us nothing but kindness and love.

Thank you to Paul Reid. Paul, as terror unfolded you chose to run in and do your best to help Saffie. We will forever thank you for staying with her until she was in the back of an ambulance.

Des. From day one you were the family's support and strength as our police family liaison officer. You couldn't have done enough for us and Xander. We were living our darkest hours and not once did you leave our side. Whatever was possible, you did it.

To Andy Burnham. Thank you for your support and opening your door for whatever we needed and allowing us to ask any concerns we had. You immediately stepped up to this tragedy for the city of Manchester and its people.

Thank you to Ariana Grande and Scooter Braun: for coming back to Manchester to organise One Love

Manchester and raising millions of pounds for those affected. What you guys did helped massively in the aftermath.

To our legal team at Broudie Jackson Canter: Elkan Abrahamson and Nicola Brook, and our barristers Pete Weatherby KC, and Anna Morris KC. Thank you all for doing your upmost to push for the truth. Your experience and professionalism throughout the inquiry was second to none.

Nicola Brook: you spent hours every day listening to us, explaining each part of what was happening during the inquiry. You went way above and beyond your job description to support us. Thank you.

Thank you Manchester Institute of Health and Performance and its physios for all the work they put into Lisa's recovery, and their work helping many of the survivors of the Manchester Arena attack.

Thank you to Once Upon a Smile charity for looking after our son Xander. Knowing he was comfortable being with you guys gave us time to grieve, and allowed Xander to voice his own concerns. Amazing work.

Thank you Humfrey at Silvertail Books, for believing in us and the book. Thank you David Collins, who had faith in the book and our story, and for wanting to write the truth, instead of believing the lies and excuses. We have laughed and cried with you. Thank you for making us feel comfortable and safe in sharing our pain.

Lisa about Andrew: thank you to Andrew, my everything, what can I say? My rock, my soulmate, my best friend. Our shared love and strength have brought us to where we are today. You still continue to amaze me with your strength and determination. Thank you will never be enough.

Andrew about Lisa: Lisa, my life and soul ... my wife. Everything started with me and you. I wish I could take it all away and make things better. Without you there is no me. You are my everything and for you, I thank you. You are the strongest warrior I know. What you went through takes superhuman strength that we all draw from each day. You are the core of our family. Love you with all that I am.

To Ashlee, Xander and Ever-Rose, who each day give us the strength to go on. We love you so very much.

Xander: you were 11 years old in 2017. What you went through that night and what you lost. You chose to become a man there and then. Your strength, love and patience got us through each day and we will forever be proud of the man you have become.

Andrew about Saffie: My beautiful daughter, you are my every breath I take and I promise you all you deserve until we are together again. I hope we did you justice in this book and explained for those who didn't meet you how amazing and special you are. You are forever in my soul x

Lisa about Saffie: Finally my biggest thank you is to Saffie. My baby. Thank you for the joy and love you filled our hearts with. Your beautiful smile, your big brown eyes, and your amazing cuddles. Thank you for the endless 'I love yous', for the love notes you would leave us, and for the family pictures and the funny memories. Thank you for choosing me as your mummy. I love you so very much. My heart and soul.

And finally: Thank you to those first responders who were in the City Room that night who stayed and tried their best to help everyone with whatever you had available under the worst circumstances possible. Always know that you tried your hardest. Our hearts are with you.

David Collins:
Acknowledgements

Firstly, I would like to thank my family for giving me the time and space to write this book. Thank you to Ben Taylor, editor of *The Sunday Times*, for asking me to produce a series of reports on the Manchester Arena attack, based on the findings of the public inquiry. This helped me get to know Andrew and Lisa Roussos. Thank you to the inquiry's transcription service (unsung heroes of public record), and countless other people, who have helped me along the way, in understanding what happened. Thank you to Pete Weatherby, for helping to explain the many things I did not understand.

This is not an easy subject, for those involved, for the city of Manchester, or for the country. But telling the story of what happened the night of 22 May, 2017, is important, I think. People should remember and understand those events. Its memory should not be allowed to fade.

I have known and met many of the families of the 22 who died over the years, and many of the survivors. Some of the people I have met along the way have found it helpful to talk about what happened, and tell their stories.

I believe this book also shows the importance of public inquiries. They can be long and expensive, yes, and their findings can be ambiguous, but they also have the power, through skilled barristers and legal teams, and judges, to at times go deeper than journalism can, compelling those were involved to give detailed witness statements, authorities to hand over documents and emails and communications, and experts to provide their opinion.

Such a record, combined with accurate and balanced journalism to piece it together, is a powerful combination for informing the public about the truth of what happened during major events, rather than relying on those with vested interests to tell us.

Thank you to Charlie Campbell, my literary agent at Greyhound Literary, for your patience, time and attention. And thank you to Humfrey Hunter at Silvertail Books, who understood, believed, and shaped this book. Humfrey had a vision, and it was the right one. I appreciate and admire his bravery in publishing this book and recognising its importance.

Andrew and Lisa Roussos are two of the bravest and kindest people I have ever met. They were a beautiful, loving, happy family, living their lives in a small Lancashire town, when they were caught up in a terrorist attack which completely changed their lives. The nation feels empathy and grieves with them, I think, because in them we see our own families. It could have been any of us who went to the concert that night.

What happened to them was not fair, and they went through unimaginable pain because of it. But I have seen that family first-hand living through that pain, and managing to live with it, against all the odds, and creating a new life for themselves. It is truly inspirational. I am grateful they trusted me to help them tell their story. I never met Saffie, but I have talked so much about her I feel like I have. She was a truly unique character. A rare spirit, who would have made me laugh.

I think about her, often.

Manchester Arena Inquiry Findings

The following passages are highlights of the Manchester Arena Inquiry findings which the author considers are relevant to Saffie's story. The full reports can be found through the links at the end of each section.

Key:
SA: Salman Abedi
HA: Hashem Abedi
BTP: British Transport Police
GMP: Greater Manchester Police
NWAS: North West Ambulance Service
GMFRS: Greater Manchester Fire and Rescue Service

Manchester Arena Inquiry Volume 1: Security for the Arena (some highlights of Sir John Saunders's key findings)

The security arrangements for the Manchester Arena should have prevented or minimised the devastating impact of the attack. They failed to do so. There were a number of opportunities which were missed leading to this failure ... SA should have been identified as a threat by those responsible for the security of the arena and a

323

disruptive intervention undertaken. I consider it likely that SA would still have detonated his device, but the loss of life and injury is highly likely to have been less ... SMG, Showsec and BTP are principally responsible for the missed opportunities. Across these organisations there were also failings by individuals who played a part in causing the opportunities to be missed ... BTP had deployed officers to police the Ariana Grande concert. They had been expressly briefed to stagger their breaks during the concert and to have concluded them by 9pm. This instruction was ignored by the officers who were present in the Victoria Exchange Complex. SA left the City Room at 9.10pm and made his way via the station concourse to a tram platform ... He waited there for a short period before making his way back to the City Room by the same route. He re-entered the City Room at 9.33pm. Because the BTP officers had ignored the instruction they had been given, there were no BTP officers in any of the public areas of the Victoria Exchange Complex during the period of SA's departure from and return to the City Room between 9.10pm to 9.33pm ... Had there been, it is possible that SA may have been seen by one or more BTP officers ... SA's return (to the City Room) presented an opportunity for him to be identified as suspicious (by Showsec security staff). This was a missed opportunity. Principal responsibility for this missed opportunity lies with Showsec, who failed to adequately train (Showsec security staff) ... At the time of the attack, SMG had in place a general written risk assessment covering its activities. It was inadequate. It failed to adapt a rigorous approach to the assessment of the risk of a terrorist attack and did not identify what steps should be taken to reduce that risk. In any event, it did not form part of SMG's planning or procedures at the time of the Ariana Grande concert.

For full version please go to
https://www.gov.uk/government/publications/
manchester-arena-inquiry-volume-1-security-for-the-arena

Manchester Arena Inquiry Volume 2: Emergency Response (some highlights of key findings)

The heroism shown by very many people that night is striking. Considerable bravery was shown by members of the public who were visiting the building, those who were employed to work at the Victoria Exchange Complex, and personnel from the emergency services. I have seen the terrible footage from the CCTV and body-worn video cameras of the scene of devastation in the City Room ... The description of that area as being like a "war zone" was used by a number of witnesses. That is an accurate description. To enter the City Room or remain there to help victims required great courage. Nothing I say in this volume of my report is intended to diminish that fact ... In addition to the individual acts of courage, there were some parts of the emergency response that worked well. Notwithstanding the concerns I expressed in volume 1 about the conduct of some in the period before the explosion, BTP officers who were present in the Victoria Exchange Complex at the time of the explosion responded immediately and rushed to the City Room. More BTP officers from elsewhere mobilised urgently. GMP also mobilised a very significant number of firearms officers and unarmed officers. There were more than sufficient rank and file police officers from GMP and BTP to assist with the response ... I am satisfied that the way in which the firearms officers acted meant that, had there been a threat from marauding terrorists with firearms, it would have been neutralised very quickly. I was impressed by the professionalism of those officers ... I have no doubt that lives were saved by the emergency response. There were many grave injuries sustained. Without the care of members of the public and those who worked at the Victoria Exchange Complex and the emergency services personnel, more lives would have been lost. While I am critical of the emergency response overall, I recognise that, at an individual level, many people did their jobs to a high standard and were a positive influence on the outcome ... It may be inevitable that when a sudden and very shocking event happens, such as the detonation of a bomb, things will go wrong. People panic ... By no means all the mistakes that were made on May 22, 2017 were inevitable, There had been failures to prepare. There had been inadequacies in training. Well-established principles had not been ingrained in practice ... Overall, and objectively, the performance of the emergency services was far below the standard it should have been. GMP did not lead the response in accordance with the guidance that it had been given or parts of its own plans ... GMFRS failed to turn up at the scene at a time when they could provide the greatest assistance. NWAS failed to send sufficient paramedics into the City Room. NWAS did not use available stretchers to remove casualties in a safe way, and did not communicate their intentions sufficiently to those who were in the City Room ... There was a lack of communication between emergency responders, both through the act of physically co-locating at a single multi-agency RVP and via radio. There was a failure to have available either a multi-agency control room talk group or to set one up on the night. This would have allowed control rooms to speak to each other directly. There was a failure by the FDO to inform other emergency services of his declaration of Operation Plato or keep it under review ... There was a failure by the FDO and others in GMP to consider zoning the scene, following the declaration of Operation Plato. Operation Plato had been declared by GMP, but not communicated to other emergency services or the unarmed GMP officers ... There were delays by NWAS in getting ambulances and paramedics to the scene. There was a failure to send all HART operatives into the City Room to assist with triage and life-saving interventions of casualties. There was a failure to send non-specialist paramedics into the City Room to assist with triage ... There was the failure to get stretchers to the City Room to help evacuate the injured. There was the failure by GMFRS to arrive on the scene and make the contribution in removing the injured that its officers could have done ... There were problems with the debriefing process after May 22, 2017. It was alarming to hear evidence that the Chief Constable of GMP had informed Lord Kerslake, during his review of the preparedness for and emergency response to the attack, that GMP could demonstrate that Inspector Dale Sexton had notified the other emergency services of the declaration of Operation Plato. That was incorrect. Inspector Dale Sexton had not done so ... The Chief Constable was not deliberately trying to deceive Lord Kerslake. It was what he had been told. It is difficult to understand how that had happened on such a crucial issue ... Temporary Superintendent Nawaz had no idea what Operation Plato was. He did not reveal this critical lack of knowledge (on the night). Instead, he gave the impression that he did know what Operation Plato was. Temporary Superintendent Nawaz should have asked the FDO to explain what Operation Plato meant ... The FDO was struggling to manage the difficult roles that he was required to fulfil. It was difficult for anyone to reach the FDO. GMP had been aware at an organisation level of the burden that would fall upon the FDO in the event of a major incident occurring since the late 1990s.

One officer described it as "an impossible task ... it would almost be like being hit by a tidal wave" ... (in his debrief) Inspector Sexton did not state that he had made a deliberate decision to conceal the declaration of Operation Plato. On the contrary, he sought to justify the failure to communicate the declaration of GMP's emergency service partners by reference to other factors, including the burden upon him as FDO ... Inspector Sexton was interviewed as part of Lord Kerslake's independent review ... He was saying that he had forgotten about the other emergency services. There is not the slightest suggestion that he had made a deliberate decision to conceal the declaration. Indeed, he was saying something quite different in the Kerslake process from what he said when he gave evidence to the inquiry ... In all of these circumstances, I am satisfied that Inspector Sexton did not make a decision on the night to conceal the fact that he had declared Operation Plato from GMP's emergency service partners. I do not consider that I can safely conclude that Inspector Sexton set out to lie to the inquiry. However, as I have made plain, I am satisfied that his evidence about the reason for his failure to communicate the declaration of Operation Plato to GMP's emergency service partners was incorrect ... Multi agency communication is vital to an effective joint-response. On the night of the attack, multi-agency communication between the three emergency services was non-existent ... By 10.50pm, the City Room was in fact a cold zone. In 2017, under the national Operation Plato guidance, a cold zone was an area where it was assessed that there was no immediate threat to life from a terrorist armed with a firearm. By 10.50pm, the GMP firearms officers were confident in their assessment that no such threat existed in the City Room.

*For full version please go to
https://www.gov.uk/government/publications/
manchester-arena-inquiry-volume-2-emergency-response

Report 3: Manchester Arena Inquiry volume 3: Radicalisation and Preventability (some highlights of key findings)

SA's radicalisation journey into operational violent Islamist extremism was primarily driven by noxious absences and malign presences. Noxious absences included a prolonged disengagement from mainstream English education and parental absence. Malign presences included the ongoing conflict in Libya and engagement with a radicalising peer group. The mosques attended by SA and HA were not an active factor or cause in their radicalisation ... The police investigation into the attack, Operation Manteline, was effective, impressive and professional. HA confessed his involvement in the attack to members of the inquiry legal team. In that confession, he revealed that he and SA were motivated by Islamic State ... There was a significant missed opportunity to take action that might have prevented the attack. It is not possible to reach any conclusion on the balance of probabilities or to any other evidential standard as to whether the attack would have been prevented. However, there was a realistic possibility that actionable intelligence could have been obtained which might have led to actions preventing the attack ... The reasons for this significant missed opportunity included a failure by a security service officer to act swiftly enough. The inquiry has also identified problems with the sharing of information between the security service and counter-terrorism policing, although none of these problems is likely to have had any causative significance ... The witnesses (MI5 officers) who gave direct factual evidence to me during the closed hearing were able to offer real insight into their thought processes at the time. On occasion, it became apparent that the security service's corporate position did not reflect what those officers did, thought or would have done at the material time. Rather, the corporate position was more by way of a retrospective justification for the actions taken or not taken.

*For full version please go to
https://www.gov.uk/government/publications/
manchester-arena-inquiry-volume-3-radicalisation-and-
preventability

In March 2024 the Independent Office for Police Conduct (IOPC) said that Chief Inspector Dale Sexton, now retired, would not face criminal charges. He will face a disciplinary hearing over evidence he gave to the Manchester Arena Inquiry. This will examine if he breached police standards of professional behaviour. This matter was ongoing at the time of writing.

Printed in Great Britain
by Amazon